COOKIES BY BESS, INC.
P.O. Box 1911
Appleton, WI   54913

Dear Friend,

It has always been my hobby to bake cookies of different types and for various occasions. During the years when my children were growing up, I accumulated cookie recipes, testing each one personally.

As a result, I compiled and classified the recipes and at the suggestion of my children and friends, decided to publish them in my first book, **Cookies by Bess.**

Now twenty years later, this book has taken on a new look. Much work, surrounded by love and affection, has gone into revising the first book.

Many new and delicious recipes have been added, also frostings, fillings, hints and short cuts on cookie baking. You will find the recipes easy to read and a joy to make.

I do hope you will enjoy as many hours of happy cookie baking as I have. My mother always said, "It is a filled to the brim cookie jar that makes happy, smiling faces from babies to grandmas and grandpas."

Happy baking always,

Bess Hoffman

CONTENTS

ALMOND COCONUT BARS

½ cup soft butter
¼ cup brown sugar, packed
1 cup sifted flour
¼ cup sifted flour
½ tsp baking powder
¾ cup chopped almonds, unblanched
¼ tsp salt
2 eggs, beaten
1 cup brown sugar
1 cup flaked coconut
¼ cup canned crushed pineapple,
   drained

Start heating oven at 350°. Mix well first 3 ingredients. Pat evenly into 9x9x2 greased pan. Bake for 10 minutes or until lightly browned. Now make this topping. Sift the ¼ cup flour with baking powder and salt. To the eggs gradually add the cup of brown sugar. Mix well. Stir in flour mixture. Mix well. Stir in coconut, pineapple, and almonds. Spread topping over baked crust. Bake at 350° 25 to 30 minutes. Cut into bars while still warm. Dust with conf. sugar if desired.

The recipes in *"Cookies By Bess"* call for all purpose flour unless otherwise specified.

SURPRISE ALMOND COOKIES

1¾ cups sifted flour
6 Tbs sifted conf. sugar
½ tsp salt
1 cup minced almond nutmeats
½ cup butter
¼ cup cream
½ tsp grated lemon rind

Cream butter, cream and lemon rind very well. Add nutmeats and mix well. Add sifted dry ingredients gradually, mixing well. Using one teaspoon of dough for each cooky, shape into a ball around a candied cherry. Bake on a greased cookie sheet in a 375° oven about 10 minutes. Will make about 8 dozen cookies.

CHINESE ALMOND COOKIES

2¼ cups flour
½ tsp salt
¾ tsp baking powder
1 cup shortening
Almonds cut in half
½ cup coconut
1½ cups sugar
1 egg
1 Tbs water
1 tsp almond extract

Cream shortening, sugar, egg water and extract very well. Add sifted dry ingredients. Add coconut. Knead dough for a few moments. Shape into small balls. Place on greased cookie sheets. Flatten with bottom of glass dipped in flour. Put ½ almond on top of each cookie. Bake at 350° 12 to 15 minutes.

ALMOND REFRIGERATOR COOKIES NO. 1

1 cup brown sugar
1 cup white sugar
¾ cup butter
¾ cup shortening
3 eggs
1 tsp cinnamon
1 tsp salt
1 tsp soda
4½ cups sifted flour
½ cup chopped almonds

Combine ingredients in order given and mix well. Form into rolls and chill several hours. Cut in thin slices and bake in 375° oven for 12 or 15 minutes.

LEMON ALMOND RAISIN DROPS

1½ cups light raisins
½ cup water

Combine the above in saucepan. Bring to boil. Reduce heat and simmer for 5 minutes. Cool.

1 cup shortening
1½ cups sugar
2 eggs
grated rind of 1 lemon
3 cups sifted flour
1 tsp soda
1 tsp salt
¾ tsp almond extract

Cream shortening and sugar until light and fluffy. Add eggs, lemon rind and almond extract. Mix well. Add sifted dry ingredients with the raisin mixture a little at a time. Drop by rounded teaspoonfuls on a greased cookie sheet. Bake at 375° 10 to 12 minutes.

ALMOND REFRIGERATOR COOKIES NO. 2

2 cups sifted flour
¼ tsp salt
1½ cups almond nutmeats, ground
1 cup butter
1 cup sugar
4 egg yolks

Mix flour, salt and nuts. Cream butter and sugar until light and fluffy. Add well beaten egg yolks and mix well. Add flour a little at a time mixing well. Form dough into 4 rolls about 2 inches in diameter. Wrap in waxed paper and chill thoroughly. Slice thin and bake on greased cookie sheets. Bake at 350 about 12 to 14 minutes. Makes about 8 or 9 dozen cookies

ALMOND TARTS

1 cup butter
2 cups flour
1 cup sour cream
2 egg yolks

Filling:

1½ cups almonds chopped fine
½ cup sugar
2 egg whites beaten stiff

Cream butter well and mix with egg yolks and cream. Blend in flour and roll into small balls. Chill dough for several hours or until firm. Press into greased tiny muffin tins. Fill and bake until a golden brown in 350° oven — about 15 minutes. To prepare filling: Fold sugar and nuts into stiffly beaten egg whites.

ALMOND CINNAMON CRESCENTS

½ cup butter
3 Tbs conf. sugar
¾ tsp cinnamon
⅓ cup chopped almonds
¾ cup plus 2Tbs sifted flour
¾ cup conf. sugar

Cream butter with 3 tbs sugar until light and fluffy. Add nuts and flour and mix well. Chill dough for easier handling. Roll into small pencil thickness logs and shape into crescents. Place on greased cookie sheets and bake at 325° for about 18 minutes. While cookies are hot, roll in mixture of the conf. sugar and cinnamon.

ALMOND APRICOT BALLS

1 cup sifted flour
½ tsp salt
½ cup butter
¾ cup chopped almonds or chopped moist coconut
about ½ cup apricot preserves
⅓ cup sugar
1 egg, separated
½ tsp vanilla

Cream butter and sugar until light and fluffy. Add egg yolk and vanilla and mix well. Add sifted dry ingredients gradually and mix. Mold into small balls. Dip balls into lightly beaten egg white and roll in chopped nuts and coconut. Place on greased cookie sheets and press top of each cookie gently with thumb. Bake at 300° about 24 minutes. While cookies are still warm, fill centers with apricot preserves. If desired, dust with conf. sugar.

ALMOND RINGS

1¼ cup butter
1 cup sugar
3 egg yolks
4 cups sifted flour
1 egg white
finely chopped almonds
sugar and cinnamon

Cream butter and sugar until light and fluffy. Blend in egg yolks. Add flour and mix until well blended. With floured hand form small pieces of dough into little rings. Dip into slightly beaten egg white, then in the chopped almonds mixed with the cinnamon. Place on greased cookie sheets and bake at 350° about 12 to 15 minutes. Remove from sheets immediately. Will make about 7 or 8 dozen.

NORWEGIAN ALMOND STICKS

1 cup butter, melted
1 egg white, unbeaten
¼ cup chopped almonds
3½ cups sifted flour
½ tsp baking powder
3 eggs, well beaten
1 cup sugar

Beat together eggs and sugar and blend in melted butter. Gradually stir in sifted flour and baking powder. Mix well. Roll out thin on floured board and cut into narrow finger length strips. Place on lightly greased and floured cookie sheets. Brush with unbeaten egg white and dot with chopped almonds. Bake at 350° for about 8 to 10 minutes.

ANGEL COOKIES

½ cup brown sugar
½ cup white sugar
1 cup shortening
1 egg
1 tsp soda
1 tsp cream of tartar
½ tsp salt
2 cups flour
1 tsp almond flavoring

Cream shortening with sugar and egg. Beat well. Add other ingredients and mix well. Roll into small balls. Dip each ball half way in water then in sugar, to form a glaze. Bake on ungreased cookie sheet in 350° oven from 10 to 12 minutes. These cookies will flatten out and spread.

FRESH APPLE COOKIES

2 cups sifted flour
1 tsp baking soda
½ tsp salt
1 tsp cinnamon
1 tsp cloves
½ tsp nutmeg
½ cup butter
¼ cup milk
1⅓ cups light brown sugar, packed
1 egg beaten
1 cup nuts, chopped
1 cup chopped raisins
1 cup finely chopped apples, unpared

Sift together flour, salt, soda and spices. Cream sugar and butter. Add egg and mix well. Stir in half of the dry ingredients. Add nuts, raisins and apples. Mix in milk and rest of dry ingredients. Drop by spoonfuls on greased cookie sheets, and bake at 400° from 12 to 14 minutes. Cookies should be placed about 2 inches apart. Frost if desired.

PAULA'S SPICY APPLE BARS

⅓ cup butter
¾ cup sugar
2 eggs
¾ cup flour
1/8 tsp salt
½ tsp baking powder
¼ tsp baking soda
¼ tsp nutmeg
¼ tsp ginger
1 cup finely chopped peeled apple

Sift together flour, salt, baking powder, soda and spices. Set aside.

Cream butter and sugar. Add eggs and beat well. Blend in sifted ingredients and mix well. Stir in peeled and chopped apple. Spread into greased 13x9x2-inch pan. Sprinkle top with mixture of 2 tablespoons sugar and ½ teaspoon cinnamon. Bake at 350° for 25 to 30 minutes. Cool and cut into bars.

4

ROLLED APRICOT TEA COOKIES

2 cups sifted flour
1 cup conf. sugar, sifted
½ tsp salt
1 cup chopped almonds
¾ cup butter
1 egg
2 tsp lemon rind, grated
Apricot jam

Mix and sift flour, sugar and salt. Cream butter. Add egg and lemon rind. Mix well. Add sifted dry ingredients with nuts and mix very well. Chill. Roll 1/8 inch thick on floured board. Cut with round cutter. Bake on greased cookie sheet at 350° for about 10 minutes. After cookies have cooled, put together with thick apricot jam. Store in air-tight container.

APRICOT BARS

1½ cups sifted flour
1 tsp baking powder
1 cup brown sugar
1½ cups quick rolled oats
¾ cup butter
1 12 oz. jar apricot jam

Mix and sift together flour and baking powder. Add brown sugar and oats and mix well. Cut in butter until well blended. Press ⅔ of mixture in 13x9x2 inch greased pan. Cover with jam. Sprinkle with remaining mixture. Bake at 350° about 30 or 35 minutes. Cool very slightly and cut into bars.

SOME SUGGESTIONS

Cool cookies on a wire rack.

Use standard measuring equipment.

Sift flour once before measuring.

Medium eggs are best.

A thinly rolled cookie will bake faster than a thicker one.

Frost cookie before entirely cool. This will give the frosting a glaze.

It's best to sift dry ingredients together before adding to mixture.

Eggs should always be at room temperature.

Use a spatula to remove cookies from cookie sheet.

Crisp rich cookies are best when stored in cardboard boxes lined with waxed paper. Other cookies will keep better in covered tins or crockery jars.

SUE'S APRICOT STRUDEL

1½ to 2 cups flour
½ pound butter
½ pint sour cream

Cut butter into flour as for pie crust. Add sour cream. Mix well. Roll dough into a ball. Wrap in waxed paper and refrigerate overnight.

Remove dough ½ hour before ready to fix. Cut dough into 6 sections. Flour board before rolling. Roll as thinly as possible.

Fill each section with the following mixture:

1 3½ oz. can coconut
1 12 oz. Jar Apricot Preserves

Roll up each of the six rolls. Bake in 375° oven for 20 minutes or until golden brown. Remove to cooling rack. Cool; then cut into one inch slices. Dust with powder sugar.

BACHELOR BUTTONS

¾ cup butter
1 cup light brown sugar
1 large egg
2 cups sifted flour
1 tsp soda
¼ tsp salt
½ cup cherries, cut in small pieces
½ cup coconut
1 tsp vanilla
½ cup chopped nuts

Cream butter and sugar until light and fluffy. Add egg and mix well. Add sifted flour, salt and soda. Mix well. Combine coconut, chopped nuts and cherries and add to mixture. Mix well. Drop on greased cookie sheets from teaspoon. Bake at 375° for about 10 minutes.

BLACK WALNUT BARS

½ cup butter
1 cup sugar
2 sq. chocolate
¾ tsp baking powder
½ tsp salt
2 eggs
¾ cup flour
1 cup black walnuts, chopped
1 tsp vanilla

Melt chocolate in pan over boiling water. Cream butter, sugar and eggs until light and fluffy. Add chocolate mixture and mix well. Add sifted dry ingredients and mix. Add vanilla and chopped nuts. Pat into greased 8x8 inch sq. pan — 9x9 inch pan may also be used. Bake at 350° for 40 to 45 minutes. Frost when cool.

BANANA BARS

¼ cup butter
1 cup sugar
2 eggs
1 cup mashed bananas
    about three medium
½ tsp lemon extract
½ cup chopped nuts
2 cups sifted flour
2 tsp baking powder (level)
½ tsp salt
Confectioners sugar icing
½ tsp vanilla

Cream butter, sugar and eggs until light and fluffy. Add sifted dry ingredients alternately with mashed bananas. Add flavoring and nuts and mix well. Spread batter in 13x9x2 inch greased pan. Bake at 350° for 30 minutes. Frost while still warm and when cool cut into bars.

For drop cookies, drop from teaspoon on greased cookie sheets and bake at 350° for 12 to 15 minutes.

BOURBON BALLS

1 cup vanilla wafer crumbs
1 cup finely chopped pecans or walnuts
1 cup powdered sugar
2 tablespoons cocoa
¼ cup bourbon
1½ Tbs light corn syrup
Powdered sugar for rolling

Mix crumbs, nuts, sugar and cocoa. Blend bourbon and syrup. Combine the two mixtures. Shape into 1-inch balls. Roll in sugar. Refrigerate. Makes about 4 dozen. They look so good served in Bon Bon cups!

BRAZIL NUT COOKIES

1 cup butter
1 cup sugar
2 eggs
2¼ cups flour
¼ tsp salt
½ tsp baking soda
2 cups chopped brazil nuts
½ cup moist coconut
½ tsp vanilla

Cream shortening and sugar until light and fluffy. Add eggs and beat. Add vanilla, nuts and coconut to above mixture, and mix well. Add sifted dry ingredients. Mix well. Drop on greased cookie sheets and bake at 350° 12 to 15 minutes.

BRAZIL NUT DATE CHEWS

1 cup pitted dates
1 whole egg
1 egg white
1 cup brown sugar packed
2 Tbs sifted flour
½ cup flaked coconut
⅓ cup sliced brazil nuts
1 tsp vanilla
¼ cup soft butter
½ cup brown sugar
½ tsp instant coffee
½ tsp vanilla
1 egg yolk
1 cup flour sifted
1 tsp baking powder
½ tsp salt

Cut dates into small pieces. Add whole egg, the egg white, the 1 cup brown sugar, 2 Tbs flour, coconut, brazil nuts and 1 tsp vanilla. Beat well. Set aside until preparing cookie base.

Cookie Base:

Cream butter, ½ cup sugar, the instant coffee, vanilla and egg yolk together until well blended. Sift in 1 cup flour, baking powder and salt together into creamed mixture. Mix to resemble crumbs. Press into well greased 9x9x2 inch pan, evenly. Spread the date nut mixture evenly over crumb layer. Bake at 350° for about 25 minutes. Loosen with small knife and turn out on wire rack to cool. Cut into small bars or squares when cool. Dust with conf. sugar if desired.

Use pan size specified in recipe.

BROWN EYED SUSANS

½ cup butter
½ cup shortening
3 Tbs sugar
1 tsp almond extract
2 cups sifted flour
½ tsp salt
1½ cups conf. sugar
2 Tbs cocoa sifted
2 Tbs hot water
½ tsp vanilla
Almond halves

Cream butter and shortening. Add sugar, almond extract, flour and salt. Mix well. Roll level tablespoonfuls of dough into balls. Place on greased cookie sheets. Flatten lightly with bottom of glass dipped in conf. sugar. Bake at 400° for about 10 to 12 minutes. Cool and frost as follows:

Combine conf. sugar and cocoa. Add hot water and vanilla. Place ½ tsp frosting on each cookie. Top each with a half almond. Let set, then store.

BROWN RIM COOKIES

1 cup shortening
1 tsp salt
1½ tsp vanilla
⅔ cup sugar
2 eggs, beaten
2½ cups flour sifted

Cream shortening, salt and vanilla until light and fluffy. Add eggs. Beat well. Add sugar. Beat for two minutes. Add flour. Mix well. Drop from teaspoon on greased cookie sheet. Press down with small glass that has been covered with a damp cloth. Decorate with ¼ of a cherry. Bake at 375° 8 to 10 minutes.

BROWN SUGAR COOKIES

1⅓ cup brown sugar
   firmly packed
⅓ cup shortening
⅓ cup butter
2 eggs
1 tsp soda
2 tsp cream of tartar
¼ tsp salt
1 tsp vanilla
3 cups sifted flour

Cream first 4 ingredients very well. Add vanilla. Add sifted dry ingredients and mix well. Roll ¼ inch thick on floured board and cut with cookie cutters. Bake in 375° to 400° oven for 8 to 10 minutes.

JANET'S BROWN SUGAR DROPS

1 cup butter
½ cup brown sugar, packed tightly
1 egg yolk
1 tsp vanilla
2 cups sifted flour
¼ tsp salt
1 cup pecans, ground
½ cup candied cherries, cut into small
   pieces

Cream butter; add sugar gradually. Beat in egg yolk. Blend in remaining ingredients. Drop from teaspoon onto greased cookie sheets. Bake at 350° for 15 to 18 minutes. Makes 5½ to 6 dozen.

Follow recipe — do not substitute unless recipe calls for a substitute.

RICH BROWNIES NO. 2

3 eggs
1½ cups sugar
½ cup shortening
1 tsp vanilla
Pinch of salt
¾ cup flour
¾ tsp baking powder
½ cup milk
½ cup chopped nuts
2 sq. chocolate

Beat eggs until frothy and add sugar, beating well. Melt chocolate and shortening over hot water and add to above mixture. Mix well. Add sifted flour, baking powder and salt, with milk and vanilla. Beat well. Spread very thinly on greased jelly roll pan. Bake in 325° oven for 30 minutes. Dust with conf. sugar or frost with your favorite chocolate frosting. Cut when cool.

BROWNIES NO. 1

½ cup shortening
2 sq. chocolate
¾ cup flour
½ tsp baking powder
Chopped nuts
½ tsp salt
2 eggs
1 cup sugar
1 tsp vanilla

Melt chocolate and shortening together. Cool. Beat eggs and sugar well. Add chocolate mixture. Mix well. Add flour, vanilla and nuts. Mix well. Pour into 8 or 9 inch square pan, greased and floured. Bake at 350° 35 minutes. Cool and dust with powdered sugar. Cut into 1 inch squares.

FROSTED PARTY BROWNIES

1 cup butter
4 sq. chocolate
1½ cups sifted flour
1 tsp baking powder
1 tsp salt
4 eggs
2 cups sugar
2 tsp vanilla
1½ cups chopped nuts

Melt butter and chocolate. Beat eggs, add sugar and chocolate mixture. Mix well. Add other ingredients and mix well. Bake on a greased jelly roll pan 350° 30 to 35 minutes. Frost with chocolate frosting. Cut into 1 or 2 inch squares.

BUTTER PUFF BALLS

5 cups sifted flour
1 cup butter
1 cup shortening
1 cup dark brown sugar
1½ tsp vanilla

Cream butter and shortening well. Add sugar and beat until light and fluffy. Add vanilla. Gradually add all the flour and mix well. Shape into small balls about 1 inch in diameter. Place on lightly greased cookie sheets and bake at 350° from 15 to 20 minutes. While still warm, roll in powdered sugar.

LITTLE NUTMEG BUTTER BALLS

1 cup butter
½ cup granulated sugar
1 tsp vanilla
¾ cup sifted conf. sugar
1⅓ cup almond nutmeats ground
2 cups sifted flour
2 tsp nutmeg

Cream butter and granulated sugar until light and fluffy. Add vanilla and nuts and mix. Add flour and mix well. Shape into small balls. Bake on greased cookie sheets at 300° about 25 minutes. While cookies are still hot, roll them in mixture of ¾ cup conf. sugar and 2 tsp nutmeg.

MAUDE'S BUTTER COOKIE RECIPE

2 cups butter
5 tsp baking powder
1¾ cup sugar
3 tsp vanilla
5 eggs
7 cups flour

Cream butter and sugar until light and fluffy. Add eggs and mix well. Add vanilla. Add flour sifted with baking powder and mix well. Separate dough into two or three parts and add a little vegetable coloring — any color you wish. Roll out on floured board about ¼ inch and brush with egg white. Sprinkle chopped nuts on top, or any other decoration. Bake at 350° to 375° from 15 to 20 minutes.

MOM'S BUTTER COOKIES

1½ cups butter
1 cup sugar
3 egg yolks
1 tsp vanilla
3 cups sifted flour
½ tsp salt
thick peach or apricot jam

Cream butter and sugar until light and fluffy. Add yolks one at a time beating after each addition. Add vanilla. Add sifted dry ingredients and blend well. Form into small balls and place on ungreased cookie sheets. Make depression in center of dough and place a little jam in center. Bake at 400° about 10 minutes. Dust with powdered sugar while still warm.

BUTTER FOR BEST FLAVOR: There is no substitute for butter. Shortening is good for some recipes.

BUTTER CUT-OUTS

1 cup butter
1 egg
¼ tsp salt
2 tsp baking powder
1 tsp vanilla
1 cup finely chopped nuts
¾ cup sugar
2½ cups flour

Cream butter and sugar until light and fluffy. Add egg and beat well. Add sifted dry ingredients, a little at a time. Add vanilla and mix well. Add nuts. Chill for several hours. Roll about 1/8 inch thick on floured board. Cut into desired shapes with small cutter. Decorate with candy sprinkles. Bake on ungreased cookie sheets at 400° about 8 or 9 minutes — just till edges start to brown.

CRISP BUTTER DROPS

2 cups sifted flour
½ tsp salt
1 cup butter
1 cup sugar
1 cup dry shredded coconut
2 eggs
1 tsp vanilla
⅔ cup chopped nuts
⅔ cup chopped light raisins

Cream butter and sugar until light and fluffy. Add eggs and extract and mix well. Add nuts, raisins and coconut and mix. Add sifted dry ingredients and mix well. Chill thoroughly. Drop by spoonfuls on greased cookie sheets. Bake at 325° for about 18 minutes. Store in air-tight container. Makes about 5 dozen.

RICH BUTTER COOKIES

1 cup butter
1 tsp vanilla
½ cup sugar
3 egg yolks
2½ cups flour
¼ tsp baking powder
1/8 tsp salt

Cream butter, add egg yolks, vanilla and sugar and mix until light and fluffy. Add sifted flour and baking powder and mix well. Chill dough. Shape into small balls and dip in ground nuts. Place ¼ of a gum drop into center of each cookie. Bake on greased cookie sheets at 375° 10 to 12 minutes. Can also be rolled, and made into sandwich cookies.

LITTLE BUTTER BALLS

2 cups sifted flour
1 tsp baking powder
¾ cup butter
1 tsp vanilla extract
1 cup brown sugar
   sifted and packed
1 egg

Cream butter and brown sugar until light and fluffy. Add well beaten egg and vanilla and mix very well. Add sifted dry ingredients gradually and mix well. Chill thoroughly. Form into small balls and roll in granulated sugar. Place on greased cookie sheets and press a nutmeat in center of each cookie. Bake at 350° for about 15 minutes. Makes from 3 to 4 dozen.

BUTTER CUT-OUTS

1 cup butter
1 egg
¼ tsp salt
2 tsp baking powder
1 tsp vanilla
1 cup finely chopped nuts
¾ cup sugar
2½ cups flour

Cream butter and sugar until light and fluffy. Add egg and beat well. Add sifted dry ingredients, a little at a time. Add vanilla and mix well. Add nuts. Chill for several hours. Roll about 1/8" thick on floured board. Cut into desired shapes with small cutter. Decorate with candy sprinkles. Bake on ungreased cookie sheets at 400° about 8 or 9 minutes — just till edges start to brown.

BUTTER NUT SWEDISH COOKIES

1 cup butter
½ cup sugar
1 egg yolk
1 Tbs cream
1 tsp vanilla
2 cups sifted flour
½ tsp baking powder
1 egg white
½ cup chopped pecans

Cream butter and add the sugar. Add the egg yolk and cream and vanilla and mix well. Add the sifted flour with baking powder. Mix well. Add the chopped nuts. Form dough into small balls size of a walnut and dip in egg white, then chopped pecans. Using little finger, make small depression in center of cookie, after they have been placed on an ungreased cookie sheet. Put a piece of cherry or any trimming you desire in center. Bake at 350° for 20 minutes.

BUTTERSCOTCH COCONUT COOKIES

1 cup butter or part shortening
2 cups brown sugar
2 eggs
1 tsp vanilla
2 cups shredded coconut
4 cups sifted flour
1 tsp baking soda
1 tsp cream of tartar
½ tsp salt

Cream butter or other fat with sugar until light and fluffy. Add coconut and mix well. Add eggs and vanilla and mix well. Add sifted dry ingredients with nuts and mix thoroughly. Shape into rolls. Wrap in waxed paper and chill until firm. Slice thin and bake on ungreased cookie sheets at 400° 8 to 10 minutes.

For Butterscotch Chocolate Nut Cookies add 3 squares unsweetened melted chocolate to fat and sugar mixture. Omit coconut and add 1 cup chopped nuts. Bake as above.

CARAMEL NUT COOKIES

1 cup soft shortening
2 cups dark brown sugar sifted
   and packed
2 eggs
1 tsp vanilla
3½ cups sifted flour
½ tsp salt
1 tsp soda
1 cup chopped nuts

Cream shortening and sugar until light and fluffy. Add eggs and vanilla and beat until smooth. Add sifted dry ingredients and mix well. Add chopped nuts and blend. Shape into rolls and chill. Slice about 1/8 inch thick. Bake on greased cookie sheets at 400° about 8 to 10 minutes.

CEREAL DELIGHTS

1 cup butter or shortening
1 cup granulated sugar
1 cup light brown sugar
2 eggs
1½ tsp vanilla
2 cups sifted flour
1 tsp salt
½ tsp baking powder
2 cups corn flakes
2 cups oat meal (quick)
1 cup chopped nuts

Cream butter and sugars until light and fluffy. Add eggs and vanilla and mix well. Add sifted flour, salt and baking powder and mix well. Add cereal and oats and mix very well. Chill if necessary for easier handling. Form into small balls and place on greased cookie sheets and bake at 350° for about 12 to 13 minutes. Press with fork before baking.

CHERRY CHOCO SURPRISES

1 cup butter
½ cup sifted conf. sugar
2 tsp vanilla
2-6 ounce packages semi-sweet
   chocolate bits
2 cups sifted flour
½ tsp salt
1 cup quick rolled oats
1 cup chopped nuts
¼ cup milk

Mix flour, salt and rolled oats together. Cream butter and sugar until light and fluffy. Add vanilla and mix. Add flour mixture slowly and mix well. Shape into finger-like cookies about 2 inches long. Bake on greased cookie sheets at 325° about 25 minutes. Cool and frost with mixture of melted chocolate bits and milk. Sprinkle with nuts.

CHERRY COOKIES

Use same method as for above cookies. Shape small amounts of dough into round balls pressing a candied cherry in center, making sure all of the cherry is covered.

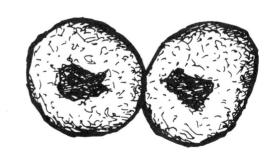

CHERRY BUTTER BALLS

¾ cup butter
1 cup light brown sugar firmly packed
1 egg beaten
1 tsp vanilla
¾ tsp baking powder
2 cups sifted flour
½ cup sugar
candied cherries cut in quarters

Cream butter and sugar until light and fluffy. Add egg and vanilla mixing well. Sift together baking powder and flour and add to creamed mixture. Mix well. Shape into balls size of a marble and dip into sugar. Place about 2 inches apart on a greased cookie sheet. Decorate with cherries. Bake at 400° for about 10 minutes or until lightly browned.

CHERRY COOKIES

½ cup butter
½ cup shortening
½ cup sugar
1 egg
1 tsp almond extract
2¼ cups flour

Cream butter, shortening and sugar well. Add egg and almond extract and mix well. Add flour mixing well. Shape into small balls. Press into each ½ or 1 whole maraschino cherry. Bake on greased cookie sheets 350° to 375° about 10 minutes.

CHINESE CHEWS

Cream:
½ cup butter
Add:
1 cup flour

Pat in greased 8 inch sq. pan. Bake at 350° for 15 minutes.

Beat:
2 eggs
1 cup brown sugar
½ cup white sugar
1 cup chopped nuts
½ tsp vanilla

Mix well. Spread on baked crust. Bake 25 minutes longer at same temperature. Cut in bars when cool.

DELICIOUS CHOCOLATE TEAS

2 cups sifted flour (cake)
½ tsp salt
½ cup butter
1 cup sugar
2 Tbs milk
1 egg
2 ounces melted unsweetened
   chocolate, cooled
1 tsp vanilla

Cream butter well. Add sugar gradually and beat until very light and fluffy. Add egg and chocolate and mix well. Add extract to milk. Add to above mixture. Add sifted dry ingredients a little at a time. Mix well. Using a cookie press, form into desired shapes. Bake on greased cookie sheets at 400° about 10 minutes. Makes about 6 or 7 dozen.

VIENNA CHOCOLATE PARTY CAKES

¾ cup butter
1 cup sugar
5 eggs
2 sq. bitter chocolate, melted
1½ cup flour
3 tsp baking powder

Cream the butter and sugar well. Add the beaten egg yolks and beat well. Add the sifted dry ingredients and the chocolate, mixing well. Fold in stiffly beaten egg whites. Fill small greased muffin tins about half full. Bake in 350° oven for 15 minutes. When cool cut through the cake and fill with apricot jam. Dust with conf. sugar.

CHOCOLATE STRIPES

¼ cup butter
⅔ cup sugar
1½ sq. melted chocolate
1 cup ground almonds
4 egg yolks
4 egg whites
½ cup flour

Melt butter, add the chocolate and the sugar. Add the ground almonds and mix well. Mix in the beaten egg yolks and the flour. Fold in the stiffly beaten egg whites. Spread ½ inch thick on well greased jelly roll sheet and bake at 350° about 15 minutes. Cool slightly and sprinkle with conf. sugar.

CHOCOLATE THUMBPRINT COOKIES

1 cup soft butter
½ cup sugar
1 egg yolk
½ tsp vanilla
1 oz. unsweetened chocolate, melted
2 cups sifted flour
¼ tsp salt
¾ cup chopped nuts

Cream until light and fluffy, butter, sugar, egg yolk, vanilla and melted chocolate. Add flour and salt. Mix well. Roll small amounts of dough into balls. Dip into slightly beaten egg white and then in chopped nuts or sugar. Place on lightly greased cookie sheets and press thumb in center of each. Bake at 350° for 10 to 12 minutes. Fill cooked thumbprints with icing or candied fruit.

CHOCOLATE SNOWBALLS NO. 2

1¼ cups butter
⅔ cup sugar
1 tsp vanilla
2 cups flour
1/8 tsp salt
½ cup cocoa
2 cups finely chopped pecans
Conf. sugar

Cream butter and sugar until light and fluffy. Add vanilla. Add sifted flour, salt and cocoa. Add nuts and mix well. Chill for several hours. Form into balls size of a marble. Place on ungreased cookie sheets and bake at 350° for about 20 minutes. Cool and roll in conf. sugar.

CHOCOLATE STARS

1½ cups sifted flour
1½ cups grated almond nutmeats
1 tsp grated lemon rind
1 cup butter
1½ cups sugar
2 eggs
4 ounces unsweetened chocolate, melted and cooled

Mix flour, nutmeats and lemon rind. Cream butter and sugar until light and fluffy. Add well beaten egg yolks and chocolate and mix well. Add flour mixture, mixing well. Roll on floured board 1/8 inch thick, using a star cutter. Bake on greased cookie sheets in 350° oven about 8 minutes.

CHOCOLATE: Always add melted chocolate when cool.

RICH CHOCOLATE SNOWBALLS NO. 1

1 cup butter
1 cup sugar
1 egg
1 tsp vanilla
2 cups sifted flour
1 tsp salt
¼ cup chopped nuts
1 sq. unsweetened chocolate, melted

Cream butter and sugar until light and fluffy. Add egg, vanilla and melted chocolate. Mix well. Add sifted dry ingredients and nuts and mix well. Form into small balls size of a walnut. Place on ungreased cookie sheets and bake at 375° for 12 to 15 minutes. Roll in powdered sugar while warm.

CHOCOLATE SHOT ROUNDS

1 cup butter
1 cup conf. sugar
2 tsp vanilla
1½ cups sifted flour
½ tsp soda
1 cup rolled oats, uncooked
chocolate shots

Cream butter, add sugar gradually and cream until fluffy. Add vanilla, flour sifted with soda and add rolled oats. Mix thoroughly, chill for about one half hour. Shape into rolls 1¼ inches in diameter. Coat each roll of dough with chocolate shots. Slice about ¼ inch thick and place on ungreased baking sheet. Bake in slow oven 325° for 25 to 30 minutes. Yield: about 4 to 5 dozen.

CHOCO-ORANGE COOKIES

1 cup butter
½ cup sugar
½ cup light brown sugar firmly packed
2 Tbs orange juice
1 Tbs grated orange rind
1 egg beaten
2¾ cups sifted flour
½ tsp salt
¼ tsp baking soda
2 ounces semi-sweet chocolate, grated

Cream butter and sugars until light and fluffy. Add orange juice and rind and egg. Mix well. Add sifted flour, salt and soda together. Add to orange mixture. Blend in grated chocolate. Shape into rolls about 1½ inches in diameter and wrap in waxed paper. Chill overnight. Slice about 1/8 inch thick and place on greased cookie sheets and bake in a 375° oven for 10 to 12 minutes.

CHOCOLATE BON BON COOKIES

½ cup butter
1 cup brown sugar
1 egg, well beaten
2 cups flour
½ tsp vanilla
1 cup chopped nuts
¼ tsp salt
¼ tsp soda
½ cup sour milk or buttermilk
2 ounces unsweetened chocolate, melted

Cream butter and sugar until light and fluffy. Add egg and vanilla. Mix well. Add sifted dry ingredients alternately with milk. Add melted chocolate with nuts and mix well. Drop from teaspoon on greased cookie sheets. Bake at 350° for 15 minutes. Frost with your favorite frosting, if desired.

CHOCOLATE SANDIES

¾ cup butter
⅓ cup sifted conf. sugar
1½ tsp vanilla
2½ tsp cold water
1¾ cups sifted flour
1 cup chopped nuts
1 package (6 ounces) semi-sweet
    chocolate bits

Cream butter and sugar until light and
fluffy. Add vanilla and water and mix well.
Add chocolate bits. Add sifted flour mixed
with nuts and beat well. Form into small
balls. Bake on ungreased cookie sheets
at 325° about 25 minutes. While cookies
are still warm, roll in additional conf. sugar.

CHOCOLATE BIT COOKIES

½ cup butter
½ cup white sugar
¼ cup brown sugar
1 egg
1 cup flour
½ tsp salt
½ tsp soda
½ tsp vanilla
1   6 oz. package chocolate bits

Cream shortening and sugar well. Add
egg, mix. Add vanilla. Add sifted dry ingredients and mix. Add chocolate bits,
mixing well. Bake on greased cookie
sheets, dropping from teaspoonfuls. Bake
in a 375° oven from 10 to 12 minutes. ½
cup dark raisins may be added if desired.

CHOCOLATE DROP COOKIES

1 cup brown sugar
½ cup shortening
2 sq. melted chocolate
¼ cup evaporated milk
with ¼ cup water
1½ cup cake flour
¼ tsp salt
½ tsp soda
1 tsp vanilla

Cream shortening and sugar and mix well. Add melted chocolate and vanilla and mix well. Add sifted dry ingredients alternately with water and milk mixture and mix very well. Drop from tsp on greased cookie sheets and bake at 375° from 15 to 20 minutes. When cool frost and sprinkle with chopped nuts.

CHOCOLATE DIPS

1 cup butter
⅔ cup sugar
3 egg yolks
2½ cups sifted flour
¼ tsp salt
1 tsp almond extract
1 6 oz. package semi-sweet chocolate bits
½ cup nuts chopped fine

Cream butter and sugar until light and fluffy. Add egg yolks and mix well. Add almond extract. Add sifted dry ingredients and mix well. Using a cookie press, form into bars about 2 inches long on greased baking sheets. Bake in 400° oven for about 7 to 8 minutes. Cool. Melt chocolate over hot water. Dip ends of cookies into melted chocolate and sprinkle with nuts. Will make about 8 or 9 dozen.

CHOCOLATE DEVILS

½ cup butter
1 cup sugar
2 eggs
¼ cup milk
1 tsp vanilla
¾ cup flour, sifted
¼ tsp salt
2 sq. unsweetened chocolate, melted
1 cup chopped nuts

Cream butter and sugar until light and fluffy. Add eggs one at a time and mix well. Add vanilla. Add melted chocolate and mix well. Pour into greased 9x9 inch pan. Bake about 25 minutes at 350°. Cut into squares while still warm. Dust with conf. sugar if desired.

CHOCOLATE COCONUT CRISPS

2½ cups sifted flour
½ tsp baking powder
½ tsp salt
1 cup butter
2½ cups light brown sugar packed
2 eggs
2 sq. unsweetened chocolate melted
½ cup chopped nuts
½ cup coconut
Pecan or walnut halves

Cream butter and sugar and add eggs one at a time. Cream well. Add melted chocolate. Add sifted dry ingredients, nuts and coconut and mix well. Drop from teaspoonfuls on to greased cookie sheets. Place a nutmeat half on top. Bake at 350° for 8 to 10 minutes.

CHOCOLATE BUTTERSCOTCH SQUARES

⅔ cup melted shortening
2¼ cups brown sugar
3 eggs
2¾ cups flour
1 tsp vanilla
½ tsp salt
2½ tsp baking powder
1 cup chopped nuts
1 6 oz. package chocolate chips

Mix melted shortening and sugar well. Add eggs and beat until light and fluffy. Add sifted dry ingredients, nuts, chocolate bits and vanilla. Beat well. Spread on greased jelly roll pan. Bake at 350° 35 minutes. Frost if desired when cool. Cut into squares.

CHOCOLATE MACAROONS

¾ cup sugar
1 cup unblanched almond strips
3 egg whites
2 Tbs water
¼ lb. grated sweet chocolate
¼ tsp vanilla

Mix the sugar and water and warm for half a minute on the stove. Add the almonds and cool. Stir in the chocolate, the vanilla and the unbeaten egg whites. Drop on a greased cookie sheet and bake in a moderate oven for 15 minutes. Cool before removing from pan. Be careful in handling as the cookies crumble easily.

SOUR CREAM CHOCOLATE DROP COOKIES

1¾ cups sifted cake flour
¼ tsp baking soda
1 tsp baking powder
½ tsp salt
½ cup chopped nuts
½ cup dairy sour cream
½ of 6 ounce package semi-sweet
   chocolate bits
⅓ cup butter
½ cup sugar
1 egg

Cream butter and sugar until light and fluffy. Add egg and mix well. Add sifted dry ingredients with sour cream and mix well. Add chopped nuts and chocolate bits. Mix well. Drop by teaspoonfuls on to greased cookie sheets and bake at 350° for 15 to 18 minutes.

CHOCOLATE GINGERBREAD MEN

½ cup shortening
½ cup molasses
2 sq. unsweetened chocolate
¼ cup milk
½ tsp soda
2¼ cups sifted flour
⅔ cup sugar
1 tsp baking powder
1 tsp ginger
¼ tsp salt

Heat, but do not boil, shortening, molasses and chocolate. When cool add milk and mix well. Add the sifted dry ingredients and mix well. Roll out on floured board to about ¼ inch thickness. Cut with gingerbread cutters. Bake at 375° about 6 minutes. Cool and frost and decorate.

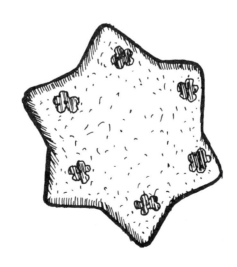

CHOCOLATE MINT DREAMS

2 cups sifted all-purpose flour
2 tsp baking powder
½ tsp salt
¾ cup shortening
1 cup sugar
1 egg
2 oz. unsweetened chocolate, melted
1 tsp vanilla

Sift together flour, baking powder and salt. Cream shortening and sugar until well blended. Beat in egg; stir in chocolate and vanilla. Add sifted dry ingredients. Blend. Shape into roll; wrap In waxed paper; chill in refrigerator about 45 minutes. (Longer chilling makes dough crack when sliced.) Cut chilled roll in 1/8 inch slices. Place on ungreased cookie sheets. Bake at 375° about 10 minutes or until slightly crisp. Cool. Spread one cookie at a time with Creamy Mint Filling; top with second cookie to make sandwich. Yield: about 40 sandwich cookies.

CREAMY MINT FILLING

2 Tbs butter
1½ cups sifted conf. sugar
2 Tbs cream
¼ tsp peppermint extract
Few drops green food coloring

Cream butter until soft; add sugar gradually, alternating with cream. Cream after each addition until well blended. Stir in peppermint extract and green food coloring.

CHOCOLATE FUDGE COOKIES

1 cup butter
2 cups sugar
4 egg yolks
2 ounces unsweetened chocolate
    melted and cooled
¼ cup milk
3½ cups sifted flour
2 tsp baking powder
¼ tsp soda
½ tsp salt
 1 tsp mace

Cream butter and sugar until light and fluffy. Add eggs and mix well. Add melted and cooled chocolate and mix. Add sifted dry ingredients alternately with milk and mix well after each addition. Roll thin on floured board and cut with cookie cutters. Place on greased cookie sheets and bake at 400° for about 7 or 8 minutes. Cookies can be frosted and made into sandwich cookies, by placing one cookie on top of one that has been frosted. Rum frosting is good.

CHOCOLATE NUT COOKIES

½ cup butter
2 cups sifted conf. sugar
4 ounces sweet chocolate grated—
    about 1⅓ cup
¼ tsp almond extract
¼ tsp vanilla
2 cups pecans, ground

Cream butter and sugar until light and fluffy. Add chocolate and extracts and mix well. Add nuts and mix well. Shape into small balls. Bake on greased cookie sheets in 350° oven for about 10 minutes.

CHOCOLATE NUGGETS

¾ cup butter
1 cup sugar
1 egg beaten
¼ tsp salt
2 sq. unsweetened chocolate melted
  and cooled
2 Tbs milk
1 tsp vanilla
2½ cups sifted cake flour
chocolate shots
chopped nuts

Cream butter and sugar, add egg, salt, melted chocolate, milk and vanilla. Mix well. Add flour. Chill. Shape into balls size of a walnut. Roll in chocolate shots or nuts. Bake on ungreased cookie sheets 375° from 10 to 12 minutes.

CHOCOLATE BAR YUMMIES

½ cup butter
2 squares chocolate
1 cup brown sugar
1 egg beaten
1½ cups sifted flour
1/8 tsp salt
½ tsp soda
½ cup milk
1 tsp vanilla
½ cup chopped nuts
½ cup coconut, if desired

Melt sugar, butter and chocolate, stirring until smooth. Cool. Add egg and mix well. Add sifted dry ingredients alternately with milk and vanilla. Mix well. Pour into a shallow greased pan. Size about 10½x15½ inches. Sprinkle with chopped nuts and coconut. Bake at 350° about 12 minutes. Cool slightly and cut into bars.

CHOCOLATE ALMOND SURPRISES

¾ cup butter
¼ cup sugar
2 tsp vanilla
Almond filling
2 cups sifted flour
½ tsp salt
4 oz. milk chocolate candy
2 Tbs milk

Melt chocolate and milk over hot water. Cool. Cream butter, sugar and vanilla. Blend in melted chocolate mixture and beat until light and fluffy. Add sifted dry ingredients, gradually. Mix well. Shape into balls, using rounded teaspoonful for each cookie. Make a hole in center of each cookie and fill with a little almond filling . . . about ¼ tsp. Seal. Place on ungreased cookie sheets and bake at 350° for 12 to 15 minutes. Roll in conf. sugar after baking.

Almond filling:

Combine ½ cup ground almonds, 1 unbeaten egg white, 1 Tbs water and ½ tsp almond extract. Mix well.

Not enough flour makes a dough that is difficult to handle and apt to spread too much during the baking period. The cookie is also apt to the porous and fragile.

Excess baking powder gives a bitter taste and produces a cookie which is too light and porous. In general, cookies take about half as much baking powder as cake. That is one half to three fourths of a teaspoon to the cup of flour.

25

CHOCOLATE ALMOND BUTTERBALLS

2 sq. semi-sweet chocolate
1 Tbs milk or cream
¾ cup butter
½ tsp salt
more sugar
½ cup sugar
2 tsp vanilla
2 cups sifted flour
½ cup chopped, blanched almonds

Melt chocolate with milk over hot water. Cool. Cream butter with salt and sugar until light and fluffy. Blend in vanilla. Mix well. Mix in cooled chocolate. Mix in flour and almonds and blend well. Shape dough into small balls; roll in sugar. Place on ungreased cookie sheets and bake at 350° 12 to 15 minutes.

CHOCOLATE LOG COOKIES

1 cup butter (softened)
½ cup powdered sugar
½ cup granulated sugar
2 egg yolks
2 tsp vanilla
3 Tbs cocoa
½ tsp salt
2½ cups sifted flour

Cream butter. Gradually add sugars. Beat in egg yolks, vanilla, cocoa and salt. Blend in flour until dough is soft and pliable using star-shaped cutter. Press dough through cookie press onto lightly greased cookie sheets. Cookies should be about 1½ inches long. Bake at 350° about 15 minutes. Use spatula to remove cookies to cooling rack. Dip ends of cookies in frosting, then in nuts, or just dust with powdered sugar which has been sifted. Recipe makes 9 to 10 dozen cookies. Freezes well.

Do not bake more than 1 pan at a time. Sometimes the baking time will depend on thickness of cookie. A thinner cookie will bake faster than a heavier one.

DO NOT OVERBAKE: Bake only until a light brown. Remove cookies from baking sheet a moment after removing from oven, unless otherwise specified.

Place cookies on wire cooling rack to avoid moisture forming.

If glaze is wanted—frost while warm. Brush tops of raw cookies with unbeaten egg white then sprinkle with sugar, nuts or colored decorating sugar. Milk can also be used to brush cookie.

CINNAMON NUT SHORTS

2 cups sifted flour
1 tsp baking powder
1 Tbs cinnamon
½ tsp salt
¾ cup sugar
¾ cup butter
1 egg
½ cup chopped nuts

Mix and sift flour and baking powder, salt, cinnamon and sugar. Cut in butter until fine as meal. Add beaten egg and nuts. Mix well. Shape into finger like cookies. Bake on greased cookie sheets in 350° oven about 16 or 18 minutes. Will make about 7 or 8 dozen cookies.

CINNAMON NUT SQUARES

1 cup butter
1 cup light brown sugar
1 egg yolk
2 cups sifted flour
1 tsp cinnamon
1 egg white
1 cup chopped pecans

Cream butter and sugar until light and fluffy. Add egg yolk and beat well. Add sifted flour and cinnamon. Beat well. Put into greased 7½x11½x1½ inch pan. Beat egg white slightly with fork. Spread over dough in pan and cover with chopped nuts. Bake at 300° about 45 to 50 minutes. Cut into squares while hot. Can dust with powdered sugar if desired.

CINNAMON LOGS

1 cup butter
1 tsp almond extract
1 Tbs cinnamon
3 Tbs sugar
2 cups flour

Mix well in order given. Shape in rolls about ½ inch in diameter. Cut in little logs about 1½ inches long. Bake on ungreased cookie sheets at 300° for 25 to 30 minutes. Cool slightly. Roll in sugar.

CINNAMON NUT TEA CAKES OR BARS

¾ cup butter or shortening
1 cup sugar
4 eggs
1 tsp vanilla
1 cup sifted flour
1 tsp baking powder
½ tsp salt
2 tsp cinnamon
½ cup chopped nuts

Cream butter and sugar until light and fluffy. Add eggs and mix well. Add vanilla and mix. Add sifted dry ingredients and mix thoroughly. Spread in shallow greased pan about 11x16 inches. Sprinkle with a mixture of 2 tsp cinnamon and ½ cup chopped nuts. Bake at 375° for about 25 minutes. Cool and cut into squares.

My family were my tasters.

CINNAMON REFRIGERATOR COOKIES

1 cup butter
⅓ cup granulated sugar
⅓ cup brown sugar sifted and packed
¼ tsp soda in 1 tsp hot water
1½ cups sifted flour
¾ tsp cinnamon
¼ cup chopped almonds
1 egg

Cream butter and sugars until light and fluffy. Add egg and mix well. Add soda dissolved in hot water. Add sifted dry ingredients and nuts and mix well. Form dough into 2 rolls about 2 inches in diameter and wrap in waxed paper. Chill. Slice about 1/8 inch thick and bake on greased cookie sheets at 400° about 6 or 7 minutes.

CINNAMON SWIRLS

1 cup soft butter
1 teaspoon vanilla
5 tablespoons granulated sugar
2 cups flour

Mix butter, vanilla and sugar. Divide flour into three parts, add one part at a time mixing well until all blended in. Using small star cutter of cookie press, make swirls or wreaths on ungreased cookie sheet. Bake at 350° for 15 to 20 minutes. While still hot, roll in the following mixture:

½ cup sugar
½ tsp cinnamon

Put on cooling rack to cool. Freezes well.

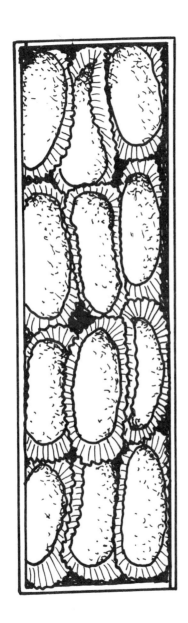

RICH COCOA REFRIGERATOR COOKIES
1¼ cups butter
1½ cups conf. sugar
1 egg
¼ tsp salt
3 cups cake flour
½ cup cocoa
1½ cups chopped nuts
4 ounces sweet chocolate

Cream butter and sugar until light and fluffy. Add egg and mix well. Add sifted flour, salt and cocoa and mix. Roll dough into rolls about 1½ inches in diameter. Roll in nuts, pressing them in on all sides. Wrap in waxed paper and chill overnight. Using sharp knife, cut into slices about 1/8 inch thick. Place on greased cookie sheets and bake in 400° oven for about 10 minutes. Cool. Melt chocolate in double boiler and frost center of cookies.

COCOA BARS
½ cup shortening
1 cup sugar
1 egg
¾ cup buttermilk or sour milk
1 tsp vanilla
1½ cups flour
½ tsp soda
½ tsp salt
½ cup cocoa

Cream shortening, sugar and egg. Stir in buttermilk and vanilla. Mix well. Add sifted dry ingredients, which have been sifted together. Mix well. Spread in greased pan 13x9x2. Bake at 350° 20 to 25 minutes. Frost with your desired frosting while luke-warm.

29

COCOA BALLS

1¼ cups butter or half shortening
⅔ cup sugar
1 tsp vanilla
1 egg
1/8 tsp salt
2 cups flour
½ cup cocoa
2 cups finely chopped pecans
Confectioners sugar

Cream butter and sugar until light and fluffy. Add egg and vanilla and mix well. Add sifted flour, salt, cocoa and nuts and mix well. Chill for several hours. Form into small balls and bake at 350° for about 20 minutes on greased cookie sheets. When cool, roll in conf. sugar.

COCONUT ORANGE COOKIES

1¼ cups sifted flour
¼ tsp baking powder
1/8 tsp salt
½ cup butter
¼ cup sugar
¼ cup light corn syrup
1 cup coconut, dry
1½ Tbs grated orange rind
¼ cup orange juice
1 egg

Cream butter and sugar until light and fluffy. Add beaten egg and syrup and mix well. Add coconut and orange rind and mix well. Add sifted dry ingredients with orange juice and mix well. Drop by spoonfuls on greased cookie sheet. Bake in 350° oven for about 12 minutes.

COCONUT PINEAPPLE BARS

½ cup soft butter
1¼ cups sifted flour
¼ cup sugar

Cut butter into sugar. Add flour and mix until crumble. Using hands mix thoroughly. Press mixture on bottom of well greased 9-inch square pan. Prick with fork. Bake in 350° oven for about 20 minutes.

Get following ready:

1 can (No. 2) crushed pineapple
   well drained
1 egg
½ cup sugar
1 Tbs melted butter
1½ cups coconut

Spread pineapple on baked crust. Beat egg and sugar until light and lemon colored. Add butter and coconut and mix well. Spread mixture on pineapple layer. Bake in 350° oven for about 20 minutes. Cool slightly and cut into bars.

COCONUT CRISPS

½ cup butter
½ cup brown sugar
½ cup sugar
1 egg
1¼ cups sifted flour
Walnut halves
1 tsp vanilla
½ tsp baking powder
½ tsp soda
½ tsp salt
2 cups corn flakes
1¼ cups flaked coconut
   (3⅓ ounce can)

Cream butter, add sugar, the eggs, and vanilla, creaming until light and fluffy. Add sifted dry ingredients; Stir in corn flakes and coconut. Mix well. Chill slightly for easy handling. Shape into small balls, place on ungreased cookie sheets about 2 inches apart. Press nutmeat half in center of each cookie. Bake in 350° oven for 10 minutes or until lightly browned. Will make about 5 or 6 dozen.

COCONUT BALLS

2 egg whites
1 cup conf. sugar
1 tsp lemon extract
1 cup corn flakes
1 cup dry shredded coconut

Beat egg whites until very stiff. Add sugar gradually, beating well. Add remaining ingredients and mix. Drop by spoonfuls on greased cookie sheets. Bake at 350° about 10 minutes.

COCONUT BARS

1 cup sifted flour
⅓ cup brown sugar
½ cup shortening
1/8 tsp salt

Sift together flour, brown sugar and salt. Cut in shortening. Press mixture into greased 8x8x2 inch pan. Bake at 375° 10 minutes.

2 eggs
1 cup brown sugar
2 Tbs flour
¼ tsp salt
¼ tsp soda
1 tsp vanilla
1½ cups chopped shredded coconut

Beat eggs slightly, add sugar. Add sifted flour, soda and salt to eggs. Fold in vanilla and coconut. Spread evenly over hot baked crust. Bake 20 to 25 minutes longer at the same temperature. Cool and cut into squares.

RICH COCONUT MACROONS

1 cup butter
2 cups sugar
1 Tbs vanilla
4 egg whites
2¼ cups sifted flour
¼ tsp salt
2 cups dry shredded coconut

Cream butter and sugar until light and fluffy. Add sifted flour and salt to which has been added the coconut. Mix well. Add vanilla. Mix well. Fold in stiffly beaten egg whites. Drop by spoonfuls on baking sheets covered with brown paper or on greased and floured sheets. Bake at 325° for about 21 minutes.

CZECHOSLOVAKIAN COOKIES

1 cup butter
1 cup sugar
2 egg yolks
2 cups sifted flour
1 cup chopped walnuts
½ cup strawberry jam

Cream the butter until soft. Gradually add the sugar. Beat until light and fluffy. Add the egg yolks and blend. Add the flour and mix well. Fold in the nuts. Spoon ½ the batter into a well greased 8 inch square pan. Spread evenly. Top with strawberry jam. Cover with the remaining dough. Bake in a 325° oven for about 1 hour or until lightly browned. Cool and cut into small squares.

DANISH COOKIES

2⅓ cups sifted flour
½ tsp cinnamon
1 cup grated almonds
1⅓ cups butter
1½ cups sugar
1 egg
1 egg yolk

Cream butter and sugar until light and fluffy. Add well beaten egg yolk and egg and mix well. Add sifted dry ingredients gradually and mix well. Chill dough. Roll on floured board and cut into desired shapes with cookie cutters. Roll about 1/8 inch thick. Brush with egg white and top with grated almonds. Bake on greased cookie sheets in 375° oven about 9 or 10 minutes. About 6 dozen.

COFFEE WALNUT BARS

2 eggs
1 cup light brown sugar
1 tsp vanilla
½ cup melted butter
1 Tbs instant coffee
½ cup sifted flour
1/8 tsp salt
1 cup chopped walnuts

Beat eggs and sugar until light and fluffy. Add vanilla and mix. Add sifted flour with salt and instant coffee. Mix well. Stir in chopped nuts and melted butter, mixing well. Pour into well greased 11x8 inch pan. Bake at 350° about 25 minutes. Cool in pan and cut into squares or bars.

JUNE'S CREAM CHEESE JAM POCKETS

½ cup butter
3 ounce package cream cheese
1 cup sifted flour
¼ cup thick jam
¾ tsp cinnamon
¼ cup granulated sugar

Cream butter and cheese. Blend in flour. Chill. Roll very thinly on floured board. Cut with 2½-inch round cookie cutter. Place ¼ tsp jam in center. Moisten edges with water. Fold over in half and press edges together with tines of fork. Place on ungreased cookie sheet. Bake at 375° for 12 to 14 minutes. Coat hot cookies with a mixture of the sugar and cinnamon. Makes about 3½ dozen.

33

DATE BARS NO. 1

¾ cup shortening
1 cup brown sugar
2 cups flour
2½ cups quick oatmeal
1 tsp soda in 1 Tbs hot water

Cream shortening and sugar well. Add soda in hot water. Add flour and oatmeal. Work to a crumbly mass with hands. Put aside ¾ cup for topping. Pack rest of batter into greased 13x9x2 inch pan. If thinner bar is wanted, press into jelly roll pan. Spread on cooked date mixture. Put ¾ cup topping on top. Bake at 350° 25 to 30 minutes.

DATE FILLING

Boil together:
1 package pitted dates
¾ cup sugar
¾ cup water

Boil until thick. Cool.

DATE BARS NO. 2

½ cup butter
1 cup brown sugar
2 eggs
½ cup sour milk
2 cups flour
1 tsp soda
1 tsp vanilla
1 cup chopped dates
1 cup chopped nuts
1 tsp lemon juice
¼ tsp salt

Cream butter and sugar. Add eggs and mix well. Add sour milk, add sifted dry ingredients, beating well. Add vanilla, add dates, nuts and lemon juice. Beat well. Spread ½ inch thick in greased shallow pan. Bake at 350° 25 to 30 minutes. Cut in bars when cool and dust with confectionary sugar.

DATE AND NUT BARS

4 eggs separated
2 cups brown sugar, packed
2 cups flour
2 tsp baking powder
¾ tsp cinnamon
¼ tsp salt
½ cup chopped nuts
½ cup chopped dates
¾ tsp vanilla

To the beaten egg yolks, add the brown sugar. Mix well. Add the sifted dry ingredients, then the dates, and chopped nuts and mix well. Fold in the stiffly beaten egg whites. Bake in a greased jelly roll pan at 350° for about 30 minutes. Frost while still warm with conf. sugar frosting. Cut in bars.

DATE SURPRISES

2 cups flour
3 tsp baking powder
½ tsp salt
2 Tbs sugar
pitted dates
3 Tbs melted butter
1 beaten egg
⅓ cup milk
1 slightly beaten egg white for glaze

Sift dry ingredients. Add the remaining ingredients to form a soft dough. Roll thin. Handle as little as possible. Cover individual dates with dough. Dates should be pitted and stuffed with a nutmeat. Glaze with beaten egg white. Bake at 350° about 15 to 20 minutes. Be sure that cookies do not touch each other.

DREAM BARS NO. 1

½ cup shortening
½ cup brown sugar
2 cups flour sifted

Cream shortening, blend in brown sugar and flour. Mix well. Press into well greased 9 inch square pan. Bake in 300° oven for 10 minutes.

TOPPING

2 cups brown sugar
1 Tbs flour
¼ tsp baking powder
2 eggs well beaten
1 cup coconut
1 cup chopped nuts

Combine brown sugar, flour and baking powder and add well beaten eggs. Mix well. Stir in coconut and nuts. Mix well. Spread over baked mixture. Bake in 350° oven for 30 minutes. Cut into bars when cool.

DREAM BARS NO. 2

Mix together

½ cup butter
½ cup brown sugar
1 cup flour sifted

Spread on greased jelly roll pan and bake in 375° oven for 10 minutes. Remove from oven and add the following.

Mix well

2 eggs
1 cup brown sugar
1 Tbs vanilla

Add
2 Tbs flour
½ tsp baking powder
¼ tsp salt

Mix well and add
1 cup chopped nuts
1½ cups coconut

Mix well. Spread on baked crust. Bake 20 minutes longer at 350°. Cut into bars when cool.

DUTCH NUT CRISPS

1 cup butter
1 cup sugar
1 egg
2½ cups flour
1 cup chopped nuts
cinnamon

Cream butter and sugar until light and fluffy. Add egg and mix well. Add sifted flour, mixing well. Separate dough into 2 parts. Press batter into two lightly greased jelly roll pans. Press nuts into batter and sprinkle with cinnamon. Bake in 350° oven from 20 to 25 minutes. Cut right away and return to oven for a few moments until evenly browned. Watch carefully.

EGG KRINGLE

⅓ cup butter
½ cup sugar
3 egg yolks cooked
1 raw egg yolk
1 Tbs hot water
2 cups pastry flour
1/8 tsp mace
¼ tsp salt
Grated rind of ½ lemon

Cream butter and sugar until light and fluffy. Add the sieved egg yolks, raw egg yolk and hot water. Sift dry ingredients and mix with creamed mixture. Add the grated lemon rind and mix well. Roll to 1/8 inch thickness and cut with a small dough-nut cutter. Bake on greased cookie sheets at 375° until lightly browned — about 10 or 15 minutes. Watch carefully.

Pastry flour is made with:
½ recipe regular flour and
½ recipe cake flour

RICH PARTY EGG RINGS

1 cup butter
1 cup sugar
6 egg yolks
Extra melted butter
Mixture of sugar and cinnamon
4 cups sifted flour
2 Tbs cream
2 tsp vanilla

Cream butter and sugar until light and fluffy. Add slightly beaten egg yolks, cream and vanilla. Blend in flour and mix well. Shape into rolls about the thickness of a pencil and about 3 inches long. Shape in little wreaths, letter S or little knots. Dip in mixture of cinnamon and sugar. Bake at 325° until golden brown — about 10 to 15 minutes. Watch carefully.

ENGLISH TOFFEE BARS NO. 1

½ lb butter
1 cup brown sugar, lightly packed
1 egg yolk
1 tsp vanilla
2 cups sifted flour

Cream butter and brown sugar; add egg yolk and vanilla, then flour. Mix well and spread on ungreased jelly roll pan. Bake 15 to 20 minutes, or until brown in 350° oven.

TOPPING

Melt one large sweet or semi-sweet candy bar (½ lb), dilute with milk and spread on toffee mixture while both are still warm. Sprinkle with chopped nuts and cut into squares.

ENGLISH TOFFEE BAR COOKIES NO. 2

1 cup butter
1 cup sugar
1 egg yolk
1 tsp salt
1 egg white, beaten until frothy
1 tsp cinnamon
2 cups cake flour
1 tsp vanilla
1 cup chopped nuts

Cream shortening and sugar, add egg yolk, add sifted dry ingredients and mix well. Add vanilla and nuts. Add just ½ cup nuts saving the rest for topping. Press dough into a greased pan about 10x15 inches. Spread egg white over dough. Sprinkle with remaining ½ cup nuts. Bake at 375° for 30 minutes. Cut into squares while warm.

FRENCH TULIES

1 cup melted butter
¼ tsp salt
1⅔ cups sugar
1 cup sifted flour
¾ cup chopped almonds
6 egg whites

Add salt and sugar to egg whites and beat with beater until soft peaks are formed. Add butter gradually and mix well. Fold in flour and nuts. Drop by spoonfuls about 5 inches apart on a greased cookie sheet. Bake in a 350° oven for about 10 minutes. Remove cookies from oven and at once roll around handle of broom or a clothes pin can also be used. Form into shape of cornucopia.

FRENCH PASTRIES

Bottom layer:

1 cup sifted flour
½ cup butter
¼ cup light brown sugar

Work ingredients together with hands and press into a pan about 7x11 or 7x13 inches. Use a floured hand to pat in place. Bake in 350° oven 10 minutes.

Top layer:

2 eggs beaten
2 Tbs flour
1 tsp baking powder
1½ cups brown sugar
1 cup chopped nuts
1 tsp vanilla

Combine all ingredients and spread over baked crust. Bake 25 to 30 minutes longer at same temperature. Cut into desired shapes at once.

FRENCH LACE COOKIES

½ cup light corn syrup
¼ cup butter
¼ cup shortening
1 cup sifted flour
1 cup chopped nuts
⅔ cup brown sugar firmly packed

Combine corn syrup, butter, shortening and brown sugar in a saucepan. Bring to a boil and remove immediately from the heat. Blend in flour and nuts gradually. Drop by rounded teaspoonfuls on a greased baking sheet about 3 inches apart. Bake in a slow oven 325° 8 to 10 minutes. Cool 1 minute. Remove carefully with a spatula. Roll cookies immediately on a clothes pin while still hot. Can also be shaped like a cone. If cookies are cold and are hard to handle, put back in oven for a moment.

FRENCH CINNAMON COOKIES

½ lb butter—1 cup
1 cup sugar
1 egg yolk
2 cups flour
2½ tsp cinnamon
1 egg white

Cream butter, add sugar. Beat in egg yolk. Add flour and cinnamon. Beat well. Roll small pieces of dough into balls. Place two inches apart on ungreased cookie sheet. Press paper thin with spatula that has been dipped in flour. Brush with egg white. Sprinkle with nuts or colored sugar. Bake at 350° 12 minutes.

FUDGE BALLS

1½ cups sifted flour
1 cup sugar
½ tsp salt
¾ cup shortening
2 sq. unsweetened melted chocolate
¼ cup coffee, cold
1½ cups quick cooking oats
chopped nutmeats

Sift together flour, sugar and salt. Add shortening, melted chocolate and cold coffee. Beat until smooth. Fold in rolled oats. Shape dough in different forms, such as balls, cones, letter S, logs. Roll in chopped nuts. Bake on ungreased cookie sheet at 350° for 10 to 12 minutes.

FUDGE COOKIES

2 Tbs butter
1½ packages (6 oz. each) chocolate bits, semi-sweet
1 can (15 oz.) sweetened condensed milk
1 cup sifted flour
½ cup chopped nuts
1 tsp vanilla

Melt butter and chocolate bits over hot water. Add condensed milk and mix well. Add flour and mix well. Add remaining ingredients mixing well. Chill. Drop from tsp on greased cookie sheet. Bake at 325° about 12 minutes. Makes about 5 dozen.

FUDGE BARS NO. 1

2 cups sugar
4 eggs
3 sq. melted chocolate
1 cup ground nuts
½ cup butter
1⅓ cup flour
½ cup milk
1 tsp vanilla

Cream butter and sugar, add eggs, add flour and milk. Mix well. Add chocolate and nuts and vanilla. Mix well. Bake in well greased 13x9x2 inch pan. Bake at 350° 35 minutes. Frost if desired. Very good frosted.

FROSTING

4 sq. melted unsweetened chocolate
4 Tbs butter
2⅔ cup powdered sugar
½ tsp salt
1½ tsp vanilla
6½ Tbs milk

Mix well. Should be of spreading consistency.

FUDGE BARS NO. 2

1 cup butter or shortening
1 cup brown sugar
1 egg separated
1½ tsp vanilla
2 cups flour
½ cup chopped nuts
1½ sq. melted chocolate

Cream butter and sugar until light and fluffy. Add egg yolk, add cooled chocolate and vanilla. Mix well. Add flour. Mix well. Spread on greased jelly roll pan. Flour hands to prevent sticking. Brush with egg white and sprinkle with nuts. Bake at 300° for 25 to 30 minutes. Cut when cool. Can also omit nuts and frost. Nuts can be added after frosting.

CATHY'S GINGER CREAMS

¼ cup shortening
½ cup sugar
1 egg
⅓ cup molasses
2 cups flour
½ tsp salt
1 teaspoon ginger
½ tsp cinnamon
½ tsp cloves
½ cup water

Cream shortening and sugar. Beat in egg and molasses. Sift dry ingredients alternately with water. Drop from teaspoon two inches apart on greased cookie sheet. Bake at 400° about 8 to 9 minutes. While slightly warm, frost with confectioners icing and top with chopped nuts. Makes about 3 dozen.

SOFT GINGER COOKIES

5 cups sifted flour
4 tsp baking powder
½ tsp salt
2 tsp ginger
1½ tsp cinnamon
1½ tsp allspice
½ cup boiling water
1¼ cups butter or shortening
1⅓ cups brown sugar, sifted and packed
1½ cups dark molasses
1 egg

Mix and sift flour, salt and spices. Cream butter and sugar beating well. Add molasses and egg. Mix very well. Add sifted dry ingredients alternately with water, mixing just enough to combine ingredients. Chill dough. Roll 3/8 inch thick on floured board and cut into desired shapes. Bake on greased cookie sheets in 350° oven for about 17 minutes.

A wonderful cookie for the little ones.

GOLD CRISPIES

2 cups cake flour
1½ tsp baking powder
½ cup butter
1 cup sugar
4 egg yolks
½ tsp lemon extract

Cream butter and sugar. Add egg yolks and flavoring. Beat well. Add sifted flour with baking powder. Chill for a few hours. Shape into small balls. Roll in mixture of cinnamon and chopped nuts. Bake at 350° 15 minutes.

GINGER CREAMS

1 cup butter
½ cup sugar
½ cup molasses
3 Tbs vinegar
2 eggs unbeaten
3 cups sifted flour
½ tsp salt
2 level tsp soda
1½ tsp ginger

Cream butter and sugar until light and fluffy. Add molasses and mix well. Add vinegar, and eggs. Mix well. Sift and add flour, salt, soda and ginger. Mixing well. Roll on floured board and cut into desired shapes with cutters. Bake at 350° about 10 minutes. Frost as desired.

GINGER BALLS

¾ cup shortening
1 cup sugar
1 egg
4 Tbs molasses
¼ tsp salt
2 cups flour
2 tsp soda
1 tsp cinnamon
½ tsp cloves
1 rounding tsp ginger

Cream shortening and sugar until light and fluffy. Add egg and molasses and mix well. Add sifted dry ingredients and mix well. Form into small balls and roll in sugar. Place on greased cookie sheets and bake at 350° 12 to 15 minutes.

GOLD COOKIES

½ cup butter
1 cup sugar
4 egg yolks
1 teaspoon vanilla
1½ cups all purpose flour
3 teaspoons baking powder
¼ teaspoon salt
½ cup nuts, finely chopped
2 teaspoons cinnamon

Cream butter. Add sugar and blend thoroughly. Add egg yolks and mix well. Add vanilla. Sift flour, baking powder and salt together. Add to creamed mixture. Mix thoroughly. Combine chopped nuts and cinnamon. Form dough into balls about the size of a small walnut. Roll in the nut and cinnamon mixture. Place balls three inches apart on greased cookie sheets. Bake at 350° about 12 to 15 minutes. Makes about 5 dozen.

DUTCH HONEY BUTTER COOKIES

2 cups flour, sifted
1 tsp cinnamon
1 cup butter
¼ cup honey
1 cup chopped nuts
confectionary sugar

Cream butter, add honey. Mix well. Add sifted dry ingredients slowly. Add nuts and blend. Form into small balls. Place on lightly greased cookie sheet. Flatten with bottom of glass dipped in flour. Bake at 325° 15 to 18 minutes. Dust with confectionary sugar while still warm.

HONEY CRISPS

½ cup butter
½ cup sugar
½ cup honey
1 egg
2 tsp grated orange rind
2½ cups sifted flour
1¼ tsp baking powder
¼ tsp salt
¼ cup chopped nuts
1 Tbs orange juice

Cream butter and sugar until light and fluffy. Add egg, orange rind and juice and mix well. Add honey, sifted flour, baking powder and salt with nuts. Mix very well. Form into 2 rolls about 2 inches in diameter. Wrap in waxed paper and chill for several hours. Slice about 1/8 inch thick and bake on greased cookie sheets at 400° about 8 or 9 minutes.

JAM BARS

1½ cups sifted flour
1 tsp baking powder
½ tsp salt
1 cup brown sugar
1½ quick rolled oats
¾ cup butter or shortening
1 cup thick jam

Sift flour, baking powder and salt. Mix with sugar and oats. Cut butter in as for pie crust. Take out ½ cup for topping. Press remaining mixture into greased pan about 7x11x1 or one almost like it. Spread with jam and spread on remaining mixture. Bake at 350° for 25 minutes.

LEMON BARS

¾ cup butter
⅓ cup powdered sugar
1½ cups flour

Blend as for pastry. Pat into ungreased 13x9x2 inch pan. Bake at 350°, 20 minutes.

In the meantime, mix the following well:

3 eggs
1½ cups sugar
⅓ cup lemon juice
3 Tbs flour
grated rind of one lemon

Pour onto hot crust. Bake at 350°, 20 minutes more. Sprinkle with powdered sugar while hot. Cut into squares or diamonds when cool.

LADY FINGERS

5 eggs
½ cup sugar
1 cup pastry flour
¼ tsp vanilla
½ tsp salt

Pastry flour is made with ½ cup cake flour and ½ cup regular flour.

Separate the eggs. Add salt to the egg whites. Beat to a foam. Add the vanilla. Slowly add the sugar, beating after each addition. Add the well beaten egg yolks. Sift the flour in slowly. Form into lady fingers on greased and floured cookie sheets. Sprinkle with sugar or finely ground nuts. Bake in 400° oven about 5 or 7 minutes. Watch carefully.

JELLY JUMBLES

½ cup butter
1 egg beaten
½ tsp soda
⅓ cup sour milk
1 cup sugar
1¾ cups sifted flour
¼ tsp salt
currant jelly

Cream butter and sugar until light and fluffy. Add egg and beat well. Mix and sift all dry ingredients and add alternately with milk. Mix well. Chill for several hours. Divide dough into 2 parts and roll dough thin. Cut with round cookie cutter and in the center of each round place ½ tsp currant jelly. Roll out rest of dough and cut with same cookie cutter. Cut two or three small openings (using a thimble) in these rounds. Place on top of jelly covered cookie and press edges together, first with fingers, then with tines of fork. Bake at 425° about 8 or 10 minutes. Watch carefully.

LEMON DROPS

2 cups sifted flour
3 tsp baking powder
¾ tsp salt
1 Tbs grated lemon rind
½ cup butter
1 cup sugar
¼ scant cup lemon juice
¼ cup cold water
1 egg

Cream butter, sugar, egg until light and fluffy. Add lemon rind and juice and mix well. Add sifted dry ingredients and mix well. Drop by teaspoonfuls on to greased cookie sheets and bake at 400° for about 8 minutes. This is a good tart cookie.

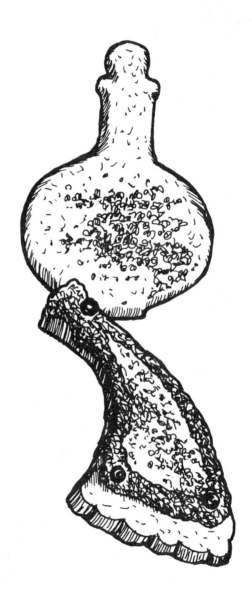

44

LEMON FLAVORED CHEESE COOKIES

1 cup soft butter
1 3 ounce softened cream cheese
1 cup sugar
1 egg yolk
½ tsp lemon juice
1 tsp lemon rind, grated
2½ cups sifted flour
½ tsp salt
colored sugar
nutmeats, finely chopped

Cream butter, cream cheese and sugar well. Add egg yolk and grated lemon rind and lemon juice. Mix well. Mix until light and fluffy. Add flour and salt. Mix well. Using a cookie press, press cookies onto a greased cookie sheet and bake at 350° for about 15 minutes. Decorate as desired.

MACROON SURPRISES

1¾ cups sifted flour
1 tsp baking powder
¼ tsp salt
½ cup chopped candied cherries
½ cup chopped nuts
1 cup moist coconut
½ cup butter
¼ cup sugar
½ tsp almond extract
1 tsp vanilla extract
2 egg whites
3 Tbs milk

Cream butter and sugar until light and fluffy. Add extracts and milk. Add sifted flour, baking powder and salt. Mix well. Add cherries, nuts and coconut and mix well. Fold in stiffly beaten egg whites. Drop by teaspoons full on greased cookie sheets about 2 inches apart. Bake at 375° about 13 to 15 minutes. Store in air-tight container.

LONDON STRIPES

1 cup butter
½ cup conf. sugar
1 tsp salt
4 eggs
2 cups flour
⅔ cup chopped nuts
1½ cups jam of your choice

Mix in order given and spread on greased jelly roll pan. Bake at 350° about 10 minutes. Spread with jam and cover with topping.

TOPPING

4 egg whites
¼ cup conf. sugar
¼ cup shredded almonds
½ tsp vanilla

Beat the egg whites until stiff. Add the sugar and vanilla and beat again. Spread on top of baked part and sprinkle with shredded almonds. Bake in 325° oven for 15 minutes. Cool and cup into stripes.

Cookies containing fruit, honey or molasses and that have a dry crisp texture, have the best keeping qualities; however, like everything pertaining to cooking, certain rules have to be followed in order to get the best results.

MANDELBRODT

1 cup cooking oil
1 cup sugar
1 tsp vanilla
4 eggs
½ of a 12 oz. jar of Maraschino cherries, drained and cut into small pieces
2 cups coarsely broken walnuts **or** 2 cups sliced almonds
4 cups flour
2 tsp baking powder
1 tsp salt

Mix oil and sugar until light in color. Add eggs and vanilla, beating well. Add nuts and cherries — mixing well with a wooden spoon. Add sifted dry ingredients in 3 parts. Mix well. This dough will be soft. Use floured hands to form into loaves about 2 inches wide and about ¾ inch high. Roll in a mixture of cinnamon and sugar. Place on greased cookie sheets — 3 rolls to each sheet. Recipe should make 6 rolls. Bake in a 350° oven about 30 minutes. Remove from oven and cut into ½ inch slices. Return to oven to toast until brown about 20 minutes. Cool on cooling rack.

MINT MELT AWAYS

1 cup butter
2 tsp water
½ tsp salt
1 cup quick oatmeal
½ cup conf. sugar
2 cups all purpose flour, sifted

Cream butter and sugar until light and fluffy. Add water and mix well. Sift together flour and salt; add to creamed mixture, mixing very well. Blend in oats. Dough will be quite stiff. Shape into little balls and bake on ungreased cookie sheets at 325° for 25 to 30 minutes. Frost when cool.

FROSTING

2 cups conf. sugar
½ tsp mint extract
¼ cup milk
green food coloring
shredded coconut

Blend together sugar, milk and coloring. Add mint flavoring. Mix well. Dip cookies first in frosting then in coconut. Place on wire rack.

MELT AWAY YUMMIES

1 cup butter
¼ tsp salt
½ tsp almond extract
½ tsp vanilla
⅔ cup conf. sugar
2 cups flour, sifted

Cream butter with salt and flavorings. Add confectionary sugar gradually. Mix well. Blend in flour, Chill. Shape into rolls ½ inch in diameter. Cut in ¾ inch lengths. Place on ungreased cookie sheet. Stamp lightly with glass that has been covered with damp cloth. Bake at 400° 10 to 12 minutes. Frost or decorate as desired.

MELT AWAY BARS

1 cup soft butter
1 cup granulated sugar
1 egg, separated
1 teaspoon vanilla
2 cups flour
1 cup chopped walnuts or pecans
colored sugar

Combine butter, sugar, egg yolk, vanilla, flour and ½ cup nuts. Blend well. Spread in ungreased 15x10 inch jelly roll pan. Beat egg white until frothy. Spread over bars. Sprinkle with ½ cup nuts and colored sugar. Bake at 350° for 25 to 30 minutes until golden brown. Cool slightly and cut into bars. Use sharp knife. Freezes well.

MOTHER'S SPICY MOLASSES COOKIES

½ cup shortening
½ cup sugar
1 egg
1 cup light molasses
4 cups sifted flour
½ tsp salt
1 tsp soda
1 tsp cinnamon
1 tsp ground ginger

Cream shortening and sugar until light and fluffy. Add egg and molasses and beat well. Add sifted dry ingredients and mix well. Chill the dough for easier handling. Roll about ¼ inch thick on a floured board. Cut with cookie cutter in desired shapes. Bake at 350° about 10 minutes. Can also be used for sandwich cookies, using a plain powdered sugar icing. Cookies should be thinner for sandwich cookies.

MOON BEAMS DELICIOUS

2 cups sifted flour
½ tsp salt
1 cup instant whole wheat cereal
2 tsp vanilla
½ lb butter (1 cup)
1 cup sifted powdered sugar
more powdered sugar

Sift flour and salt. Stir in cereal. Cream butter, add the 1 cup powdered sugar gradually and beat until light and fluffy. Add vanilla. Stir in flour mixture and beat until blended. Shape dough into 2 inch crescents about the thickness of a finger. Place on lightly greased cookie sheet. Bake in a 325° oven for about 20 minutes or until light brown. Roll in powdered sugar and cool before storing. Will make about 5 or 6 dozen.

NORWEGIAN GOODIES

1½ cups butter
1 cup sugar
3 eggs
2 Tbs milk
3½ cups flour sifted
1 tsp soda
¾ tsp salt
½ cup chopped nuts
grated chocolate

Cream sugar and butter until light and fluffy. Add beaten eggs and milk and vanilla. Mix well. Add sifted dry ingredients and mix very well. Chill. Shape into small balls size of a marble. Place on ungreased cookie sheets and flatten with bottom of glass that has been covered with a damp cloth. Sprinkle tops of cookies with grated chocolate and chopped nuts. Bake at 325° to 350° 12 to 15 minutes.

SCOTCH OATMEAL COOKIES

1 cup butter or ½ shortening
1 cup light brown sugar, packed
½ cup white sugar
1 tsp vanilla
⅓ cup warm water mixed with 1 tsp soda
2 cups sifted flour
2 cups quick oatmeal, raw

Cream butter with sugars until light and fluffy. Add vanilla and soda with warm water and mix well. Add flour and oatmeal a little at a time and mix well. Drop from teaspoon on greased cookie sheets and bake at 350° for about 15 minutes.

SOUR CREAM OATMEAL COOKIES

2½ cups sifted flour
½ tsp salt
1 tsp baking soda
2 tsp cinnamon
½ tsp nutmeg
½ tsp cloves
2 cups quick rolled oats
2 cups raisins
1 cup chopped nuts
1 cup butter
2 cups brown sugar sifted and packed
2 eggs
1 cup dairy sour cream

Mix and sift flour, salt, soda and spices. Combine oats, raisins and nuts. Cream butter, sugar and eggs until light and fluffy. Add rolled oats mixture and mix well. Add sifted flour mixture with flour a little at a time and mix well. Drop by spoonfuls on greased cookie sheets and bake at 375° for about 15 minutes. Makes about 9 dozen.

OATMEAL CHOCOLATE CHIP COOKIES

1 cup shortening
1 cup brown sugar
1 cup white sugar
2 eggs
2 tsp vanilla
1 6 oz. package chocolate chips
2 cups sifted flour
¾ tsp soda
½ tsp salt
½ tsp baking powder
2 cups of quick oatmeal

Cream shortening and sugars until light and fluffy. Add eggs and beat well. Add sifted flour, salt and baking powder and baking soda and mix well. Add the oats and mix well. Add vanilla and chocolate chips and beat very well. Drop by teaspoonfuls on greased cookie sheet. Bake at 350° about 15 minutes.

OATMEAL LOGS

½ cup butter
½ cup shortening
2 tsp vanilla
½ cup conf. sugar
2 cups flour sifted
½ tsp salt
1 cup quick cooking oats

Cream butter, shortening and sugar. Add vanilla, flour and salt. Stir in oatmeal. Shape into finger sized logs — about 1½ inches long. Bake on ungreased cookie sheet at 325° for 25 to 30 minutes. Frost with chocolate frosting when cool. Decorate as desired.

OLD FASHIONED OATMEAL COOKIES

1 cup shortening
1½ cups brown sugar
2 eggs
½ cup buttermilk
½ cup raisins
½ cup chopped nuts
3 cups quick rolled oats
1¾ cup sifted flour
1 tsp soda
1 tsp baking powder
1 tsp salt
1 tsp nutmeg
1 tsp cinnamon

Cream together shortening, butter and eggs until light and fluffy. Stir in buttermilk. Sift together flour, baking powder, soda and salt and spices. Add to creamed mixture and mix well. Stir in oats, nuts and raisins and beat well. Drop from teaspoon onto greased cookie sheets and bake at 400° for 8 to 10 minutes. Cool for a moment before removing from sheets.

CHOCOLATE OATMEAL GOODIES

1 cup butter
2 cups sugar
2 eggs
3 tsp vanilla
4 sq. chocolate, melted and cooled
1½ cups sifted flour
1 tsp salt
2 tsp baking powder
3 cups quick cooking oats

Mix and sift flour, salt, and baking powder and oats and mix well. Cream butter and sugar and mix until light and fluffy. Add eggs, vanilla and chocolate and mix well. Add sifted dry ingredients and mix well. Shape into balls about the size of walnuts. Place on greased cookie sheets and flatten with tines of fork. Bake in 350° oven about 10 minutes. Makes 6 or 7 dozen. Dads favorite.

CHOCOLATE OATMEAL DROPS

1 cup sifted flour
½ tsp soda
½ tsp salt
1 cup sugar
½ cup butter or other shortening, softened
2 oz. chocolate, melted and cooled
1 egg
1 tsp vanilla
½ tsp almond flavoring
½ cup quick cooking oats
½ cup light raisins
¼ cup walnuts, chopped

Mix flour, sugar, soda and salt together. Add butter, chocolate, egg, vanilla and almond extract. Mix well. Stir in rolled oats, raisins, and nutmeats. Drop by teaspoonfuls on greased cookie sheets. Bake at 350° for 12 to 15 minutes. Makes about 4 dozen.

PARTY FACE COOKIES

½ cup butter
1 cup brown sugar, packed
1 tsp vinegar
½ cup buttermilk
½ cup molasses
2½ cups sifted flour
1 tsp baking soda
½ tsp salt
½ tsp ginger
½ tsp cinnamon
Raisins or currants for faces.

Sour milk can be used instead of buttermilk.

Cream butter and sugar until light and fluffy. Add vinegar and mix. Combine buttermilk or sour milk and molasses. Add sifted dry ingredients alternately with milk mixture and mix well. Drop by teaspoonfuls on ungreased cookie sheets and make faces with currants or raisins. Bake at 350° 10 to 15 minutes.

SALTED PEANUT COOKIES

1 cup butter
1 cup brown sugar, sifted and packed
1 egg
1 cup chopped salted peanuts
1¼ cups flour
2½ tsp baking powder
1½ cups corn flakes
1½ cups quick rolled oats

Cream butter and sugar until light and fluffy. Add egg and mix well. Add corn flakes and oats and mix well. Add sifted flour and baking powder and mix well. Add peanuts. Drop by spoonfuls on greased cookie sheets and bake at 375° for about 11 or 12 minutes.

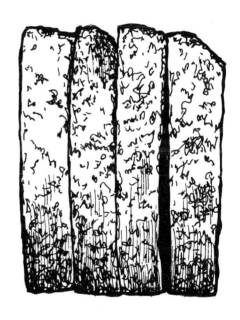

PEANUT SQUARES

1 cup shortening
1 cup sugar
2 egg yolks
1 Tbs water
1 tsp vanilla
2 cups sifted flour
¼ tsp salt
¼ tsp soda

Cream shortening and sugar until light and fluffy. Add egg yolks, water and vanilla and mix well. Add sifted dry ingredients and mix well. Spread on greased jelly roll pan and sprinkle with chocolate chips. Beat two egg whites until stiff. Add 1 cup brown sugar. Spread on above mixture and add about ¾ cup ground Spanish peanuts. Bake at 375° about 25 minutes. Cut into squares when cool.

PEANUT BUTTER REFRIGERATOR COOKIES

1¾ cups sifted flour
½ tsp salt
½ tsp soda
½ cup peanut butter
¼ cup soft butter
1 cup brown sugar lightly packed
1 egg
¼ cup evaporated milk

Cream butter and peanut butter until light and fluffy. Add sugar gradually and mix well. Beat in egg. Add sifted dry ingredients with milk a little at a time. Mix well. Shape into rolls about 2 inches in diameter. Chill overnight, wrapped in wax paper. Cut into 1/8 inch slices and bake on greased cookie sheets at 375° for about 10 minutes.

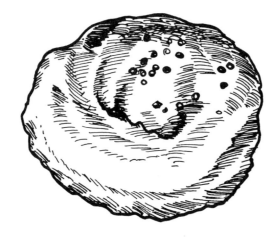

PEANUT BUTTER COOKIES

1 cup shortening
1 cup peanut butter
1 cup brown sugar
1 cup white sugar
2 eggs
2½ cups flour
½ tsp salt
2 tsp soda
1 tsp vanilla

Cream shortening, sugars and peanut butter. Add eggs and vanilla. Beat very well. Add sifted dry ingredients. Mix well. Roll into small balls. Place on ungreased cookie sheet. Press down with tines of fork. Bake at 375° 8 to 10 minutes.

PEANUT BUTTER WHEELS

½ cup butter
1 cup sugar
½ cup peanut butter, chunk style
1 egg
2 Tbs milk
1 6 oz. package semi-sweet chocolate bits
1¾ cups sifted flour
½ tsp salt
½ tsp soda
1 tsp vanilla

Cream butter and sugar until light and fluffy. Add egg, milk and vanilla and mix well. Add peanut butter, mixing well. Add sifted dry ingredients. Mix well. Place dough on a floured board. Roll into a rectangle about 15 by 8 inches. Melt chocolate over hot water and spread over dough. Roll as for jelly roll. Chill thoroughly. Slice about ¼ inch thick and bake on greased cookie sheets at 375° about 8 or 9 minutes. Use sharp knife for slicing.

SMALL PECAN DROPS

½ cup butter
⅔ cup dark brown sugar sifted and packed
½ tsp vanilla, optional
1 egg yolk
1 cup sifted flour
1/8 tsp cream of tartar
½ tsp salt
⅓ cup chopped pecans

Cream butter and sugar and egg until light and fluffy. Add sifted flour and salt and cream of tartar to which the chopped nuts have been added. Mix well. Drop by teaspoonfuls on greased cookie sheets and bake at 300° for about 25 minutes.

PECAN KISSES

2 cups flour, sifted
1 cup sugar
2 cups ground pecans
1 cup soft butter
2 tsp rum

Mix and sift flour and sugar, add nuts and mix. Add all remaining ingredients and mix very well. Using a heaping tsp for each cookie, form into balls. Bake on greased baking sheets. Bake at 300° 25 minutes. When cool, sprinkle with conf. sugar. Makes about 6 dozen cookies.

Poor cookies may result from inaccurate measurements, poor materials, improper handling and incorrect baking. Inaccurate measurement is the most frequent cause.

53

SOUTHERN PECAN COOKIES

1 cup butter
2 Tbs conf. sugar
1 cup chopped pecans
2 cups flour
1 tsp baking powder
2 Tbs ice water
1 tsp vanilla

Cream butter, add rest of ingredients one at a time. Mix very well. Roll thin on a floured board. Cut with a small round cutter. Sprinkle with sugar and bake on a greased cookie sheet 350° 10 minutes.

ORANGE PECAN COOKIES

1 cup butter or shortening
½ cup brown sugar
½ cup white sugar
1 egg, beaten
1 Tbs grated orange rind
3 Tbs orange juice
2¾ cup sifted flour
¼ tsp soda
¼ tsp salt
½ cup chopped pecans

Cream butter and sugars until light and fluffy. Add egg and orange rind and juice. Mix well. Add sifted dry ingredients and chopped pecans and mix well. Shape dough into rolls about 2 inches in diameter. Wrap in waxed paper and chill for several hours. Cut into ¼ inch slices and bake on slightly greased cookie sheets at 375° for about 10 to 12 minutes. Should be removed from sheets immediately.

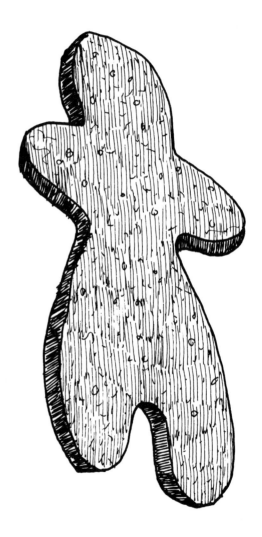

PECAN REFRIGERATOR COOKIES

1 cup butter
¾ cup granulated sugar
¾ cup brown sugar, packed
2 tsp lemon juice
1 egg yolk
1 egg
3 cups sifted flour
¼ tsp salt
2 tsp baking powder
½ tsp cinnamon
¾ cups chopped pecans

Cream butter, sugars until light and fluffy. Add lemon juice, egg, egg yolk, mix well. Add sifted dry ingredients with nuts and mix well. Form dough into 3 rolls about 2 inches in diameter and chill. Slice thin. Bake on greased cookie sheets at 400° for about 7 minutes. Dust with conf. sugar if desired.

PECAN DELIGHTS

1¼ cup butter
1 cup powdered sugar
½ cup cocoa
¼ tsp salt
1 tsp vanilla
2 cups flour
1 cup chopped pecans
Powdered sugar

Cream butter and sugar; add cocoa, salt and vanilla. Cream well. Blend in flour and pecans. Chill if dough is soft. Roll into balls the size of a walnut. Place on ungreased cookie sheets. Bake in a 300° oven for about 20 minutes. Cool. Roll in powdered sugar. Makes about 6 dozen.

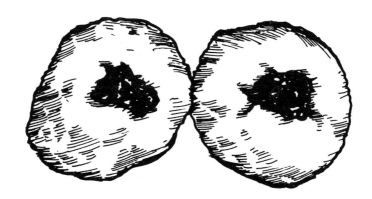

PECAN MAPLE COOKIES

1 cup butter or shortening
3 cups brown sugar
2 eggs beaten
4 cups cake flour
½ tsp salt
1 tsp maple flavoring
1 tsp baking powder
1 cup chopped nuts
3 cups coconut

Cream butter, sugar, flavoring and egg well. Add sifted flour, salt and baking powder. Mix well. Add chopped nuts and coconut. Mix well. Form into rolls about 1½ inches in diameter. Wrap in waxed paper and chill. Slice about ¼ inch thick and bake at 350° about 10 minutes.

PECAN FINGERS

1 cup butter
½ cup conf. sugar
2 cups ground pecans
2 cups flour—sifted
2 tsp vanilla
½ tsp salt

Cream butter and sugar well. Add all other ingredients and mix well. Form into rolls about 1½ inches long. About finger thickness. Bake on ungreased cookie sheets in 300° oven about 25 minutes. Cookies should be light in color. Roll in conf. sugar while warm.

PFEFFERNUESSE

4 cups sifted flour
1 tsp baking soda
½ tsp salt
1 Tbs Cinnamon
1 tsp cloves
1 tsp nutmeg
¼ tsp black pepper
1 Tbs crushed cardamon seeds
1 tsp anise oil
¼ lb. candied orange peel, ground fine
½ lb. ground citron
2 Tbs butter
2½ cups conf. sugar
5 eggs, separated
1½ tsp grated lemon rind
¼ cup milk
1 cup conf. sugar

Sift together flour, salt, soda and spices. Stir in seeds and orange peel and citron. Mix together butter and sugar. Beat egg yolks well and add to butter mixture with lemon peel. Stir in flour fruit mixture. Fold in stiffly beaten egg whites. Chill for about 1 hour. Shape with well floured hands into small balls. Place on a greased cookie sheet and cover with towel. Let stand overnight. Combine milk with 2½ cups conf. sugar. Brush cookies with this mixture. Bake in a 350° oven from 15 to 29 minutes. Store in tightly covered container to age. Dust with conf. sugar before serving. Makes about 7 or 8 dozen cookies.

Sugar in excess gives a waxy product and destroys and conceals the flavor of the other ingredients.

JOANNE'S TASTY PINEAPPLE BARS

¾ cup butter, softened
1 cup sugar
1 egg
½ cup pineapple preserves
2 cups flour
1 tsp baking soda
½ tsp salt
½ cup chopped walnuts

Cream butter and sugar till fluffy. Beat in egg and preserves. Sift together flour, baking soda and salt. Stir into creamed mixture. Fold in nuts. Spread into greased 13x9x2 inch pan. Bake in a 350° oven about 25 to 30 minutes. Cool thoroughly and cut into bars. Frost as you desire.

PINEAPPLE REFRIGERATOR COOKIES

⅔ cup butter
1 cup brown sugar, firmly packed
½ cup crushed pineapple, drained
1 tsp soda
2 eggs
1 tsp vanilla
3 cups flour
½ tsp salt

Cream butter and sugar well. Add eggs one at a time and mix well. Stir in well drained pineapple and vanilla. Add sifted dry ingredients. Mix well. Shape into two rolls 2 inches in diameter. Wrap in waxed paper and refrigerate for several hours. Slice 1/8 inch thick. Bake on greased cookie sheets in 375° oven for 15 minutes or until lightly browned.

Cookies are easy to bake and have the advantage over cakes in that they keep for several months.

PINWHEEL COOKIES

1¼ cups butter
1½ cups conf. sugar
2 egg yolks
3 cups flour
1 tsp vanilla
4 Tbs cocoa

Cream butter and sugar until light and fluffy. Add beaten egg yolks and beat well. Add the sifted flour and the vanilla. Beat well. To half of the mixture add the cocoa. Roll out each half separately into a large rectangle. Place the cocoa part on top of the white part and roll as for jelly roll. Wrap in wax paper and chill until firm. Cut into ¼ inch slices. Bake on greased cookie sheets in 400° oven for about 5 minutes.

DATE FILLED PIN WHEEL COOKIES

1 cup shortening
1 cup white sugar
1 cup light brown sugar
3 eggs
4 cups flour
1 tsp soda
1 tsp vanilla
½ tsp salt

Cream shortening and sugars. Add eggs, mixing well. Add sifted dry ingredients, mixing well. Roll ½ inch thick on floured board. Spread on date filling. Roll as for jelly roll. Divide in 4 parts. Wrap in waxed paper. Chill. Slice ¼ inch thick. Bake on greased cookie sheet at 400° for 10 or 11 minutes.

DATE FILLING

1 lb. pitted dates, cup up
½ cup water
Cook until thick. Cool.

RANCH COOKIES
1 cup butter (½ shortening)
1 cup white sugar
1 cup brown sugar
1 tsp vanilla
2 eggs
1 cup coconut or 1 cup chopped nuts
2 cups sifted flour
1 tsp baking powder
1 tsp baking soda
½ tsp salt
2 cups quick oatmeal
2 cups rice krispies

Cream butter and sugar until light and fluffy. Add eggs and vanilla and mix well. Add sifted flour, salt, soda and baking powder and mix well. Add oatmeal, rice krispies, coconut or nuts and mix well. Drop by spoonfuls onto greased cookie sheets. Dip tines of fork in milk and flatten cookies with fork. Bake at 375° for about 10 to 12 minutes.

ROSETTES
2 eggs
1 Tbs granulated sugar
¼ tsp salt
1 cup flour
1 cup milk
1 tsp vanilla
Fat for frying
Powdered sugar

Combine eggs, granulated sugar, and ¼ tsp salt. Beat well. Add flour, milk and vanilla. Beat until smooth. Heat Rosette iron in hot fat (375°). Dip hot iron in batter, being careful batter comes only ¾ of way up side of iron. Fry Rosette in hot fat until golden brown — about ½ minute. Lift iron out of fat. Tip slightly to drain onto paper towel. Place on rack to cool. Continue process to use rest of batter, reheating iron each time. Sift powdered sugar over cooled Rosettes. Makes 3½ dozen.

MOTHER'S POPPY SEED COOKIES

3 eggs
½ cup cooking oil
1 cup sugar
3¼ cups flour
¼ tsp salt
½ cup poppy seeds washed in warm
    water and drained
2 tsp baking powder
1 tsp vanilla

Beat eggs, oil and sugar well. Add poppy seeds and vanilla. Mix in sifted dry ingredients. Mix well. Roll on floured board 1/8 inch thick. Cut into desired shapes with cookie cutter. Brush with milk lightly and sprinkle with sugar mixed with cinnamon. Bake at 375° for about 10 minutes.

ROCKS

1 cup butter
1½ cups sugar
3 eggs, beaten
1½ cups dates, cut up
1½ cups pecans, chopped
2½ cups sifted flour
½ tsp allspice
1 tsp cinnamon
1 tsp soda

Cream butter and sugar until light and fluffy. Add eggs and beat well. Add sifted dry ingredients and mix well. Add dates and nuts and blend. Drop by teaspoonfuls on greased cookie sheets and bake at 400° for about 12 to 15 minutes.

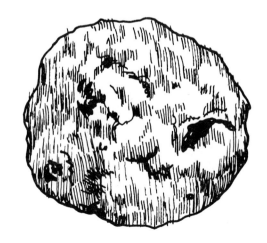

HUNGARIAN RUM BUTTER COOKIES

1½ cups butter
1 cup sugar
2 eggs, separated
1 Tbs rum
4 cups sifted flour
½ cup chopped nuts

Cream butter and sugar until light and fluffy. Beat in egg yolks and rum and mix well. Add flour gradually to make a smooth dough. Roll out on floured board about 1/8 inch thickness. Cut with cookie cutters in desired shapes.

TOPPING

Beat 2 egg whites very stiff. Drop ½ tsp egg white on each cookie. Sprinkle a little nuts on top. Bake at 350° about 10 minutes.

SANDIES

1 cup butter
¼ cup conf. sugar
2 tsp vanilla
1 Tbs water
2 cups flour
1 cup chopped pecans

Cream butter and sugar well. Add vanilla and water. Mix well. Add flour and chopped nuts, mixing well. Shape into small balls or finger sized logs. Bake on ungreased cookie sheet in 300° oven for about 20 minutes or until a light brown.

Not enough fat may result in a tough cookie with a dry texture.

SCOTCH TOFFIES

2 cups quick cooking oats
⅓ cup melted butter
½ cup light brown sugar, firmly packed
¼ cup dark corn syrup
½ tsp salt
1½ tsp vanilla
1 cup semi-sweet chocolate bits
¼ cup nutmeats

Combine all ingredients in order given and press into an 8x8 or 9x9 inch greased pan. Bake at 350° for 25 minutes. Cut in squares while warm. Dust with conf. sugar if desired.

SCOTCH SHORTBREADS NO. 1

2 cups sifted flour
¼ tsp baking powder
½ tsp salt
1 cup butter
½ cup sifted conf. sugar

Cream butter and sugar until light and fluffy. Knead in sifted dry ingredients. Roll ⅓ inch thick on floured board. Cut into desired shapes. Bake on lightly greased cookie sheets in 350° oven about 20 minutes. Should be a delicate brown.

SCOTCH SHORTBREADS NO. 2

3 cups flour
2 cups butter
1 cup powdered sugar
1½ tsp vanilla

Cream butter and sugar and vanilla until light and fluffy. Add flour and mix well. Roll out on lightly floured board. Cut with cookie cutters. Bake at 375° about 15 minutes. When cool can be frosted with any frosting. Makes a wonderful holiday cookie.

SESAME SEED COOKIES

1 cup butter
1 cup sugar
2 eggs beaten
½ cup water
3 cups sifted flour
2 tsp baking powder
½ tsp salt
2 tsp sesame seeds

Cream butter and sugar until light and fluffy. Add beaten eggs and water and mix well. Add sifted flour, baking powder and salt. Mix well. Sprinkle in sesame seeds. Mix. Chill. Roll thin on floured board. Cut with a small round glass or cutter dipped in flour. Bake at 325° for about 15 minutes.

SHERRY NUT DROP COOKIES

1½ cups butter
1¾ cups sifted conf. sugar
1 cup chopped pecans
3⅓ cups flour, sifted
¼ tsp salt
½ cup sweet sherry wine

Cream butter and sugar until light and fluffy. Add chopped nuts and mix well. Add sifted dry ingredients with wine and mix well. Drop by spoonfuls on lightly greased cookie sheets and bake at 350° for about 18 or 20 minutes.

Excess fat makes the dough difficult to handle, and may result in a cookie with a greasy texture and poor flavor.

SHORT BREAD BALLS

1 cup butter
¼ cup sugar
¾ tsp salt
1 tsp vanilla
2 cups sifted flour
1 cup pecans, chopped

Cream butter and sugar. Blend in remaining ingredients and mix well. This dough will be soft. Form into small balls. Bake on ungreased cookie sheets in slow oven 300° 30 to 40 minutes or until slightly browned. Roll in conf. sugar while still warm. Use floured hands to form into balls.

SNICKERDOODLES

1 cup soft butter
1½ cups sugar
2 eggs
2 Tbs cinnamon
2 Tbs sugar
2¾ cups sifted flour
2 tsp cream of tartar
1 tsp baking soda
½ tsp salt

Cream butter and sugar and eggs. Stir in sifted dry ingredients. Mix well. Chill dough. Roll into small balls and in mixture of the 2 Tbs cinnamon and 2 Tbs sugar. Place about 2 inches apart on greased cookie sheets. Bake in 400° oven until lightly browned and still soft. About 8 or 10 minutes. These cookies will puff up and then flatten out.

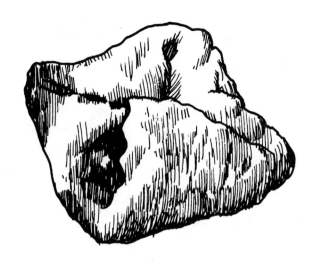

SPICE COFFEE DROPS

½ cup shortening
1 cup brown sugar, packed
1 egg
6 Tbs cold coffee
½ cup chopped nuts
1 cup chopped dates
2 cups sifted flour
½ tsp baking powder
½ tsp baking soda
½ tsp cinnamon
¼ tsp salt
¼ tsp nutmeg

Cream shortening and sugar until light. Add egg and beat well. Add sifted dry ingredients and add to creamed mixtures, alternating with the coffee. Add dates and nuts. Mix well. Drop by spoonfuls (tsp) on greased cookie sheets. Bake at 400° for 9 to 10 minutes. Will make 5 to 6 dozen.

FROSTED SPICE BARS

2 cups light brown sugar
1 cup shortening
1 cup cold coffee
1 cup raisins
3 cups sifted flour
1 tsp soda
1 tsp baking powder
1 tsp cinnamon
1 tsp nutmeg
2 eggs

Cream shortening, add sugar and eggs and beat well. Add sifted dry ingredients with coffee. Mix well. Spread thinly on two greased cookie sheets. Bake at 350° about 25 to 30 minutes or until cake pulls away from pan. Frost with your favorite frosting while warm. Cut into desired shapes when cool.

SOUR CREAM COOKIES NO. 1

1 cup butter
1 cup sugar
3 cups flour
1 tsp salt
1 tsp soda
1 tsp nutmeg
1 egg well beaten
1 cup sour cream

Sift dry ingredients, add butter. Work in with pastry blender. Add egg. Mix well. Add part of sour cream to mixture. Mix well. Add rest of cream. This will make a soft dough. Chill for one hour. Roll on floured board. Cut in desired shapes. Sprinkle with sugar. Bake at 400° 10 minutes.

SOUR CREAM COOKIES NO. 2

2⅔ cups sifted flour
½ tsp baking soda
1 tsp baking powder
1 tsp nutmeg
1 cup butter
1 cup sugar
1 egg
½ cup sour cream

Cream butter and sugar and mix well. Add sifted dry ingredients with sour cream. Mix just enough for each addition to com- Mix just enough after each addition to combine ingredients. Chill dough about 2½ hours. Roll thin on floured board. Cut into desired shapes with cookie cutter. Bake on greased cookie sheets 375° about 10 minutes. Will make about 13 or 14 dozen.

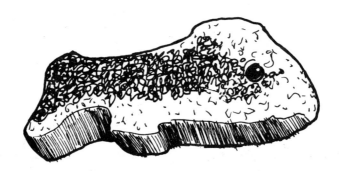

SPICE SPECIALS

2 cups sifted flour
¾ tsp cinnamon
½ tsp cloves
1 cup butter
1 cup sugar
2 egg yolks
1 cup grated almonds
1 tsp lemon rind

Mix and sift flour and spices. Cream butter and sugar until light and fluffy. Add unbeaten egg yolks, nuts and lemon rind. Mix well. Add sifted dry ingredients. Roll ¼ inch thick on lightly floured board. Cut with scalloped cutter. Bake on greased cookie sheet 350° 13 to 15 minutes.

Swedish

CHOCOLATE SPRITZ

1 cup butter
2 cups sugar
2 eggs
4 Tbs milk
4 cups sifted cake flour
½ tsp salt
4 squares unsweetened chocolate,
    melted and cooled

Cream butter and sugar until light and fluffy. Add eggs and mix well. Add sifted flour and salt with milk, a little at a time and mix well. Add cooled chocolate and mix. Using cookie press for desired shapes, form on ungreased cookie sheets. Bake at 375° for 10 to 12 minutes.

SPRITZ COOKIES

3 cups sifted cake flour
½ tsp baking powder
¼ tsp salt
1 cup butter
¾ cup sugar
3 egg yolks
1 tsp almond extract

Cream butter and sugar until light and fluffy. Add beaten egg yolks and almond extract. Mix well. Add sifted dry ingredients gradually and mix. Chill thoroughly. Using cookie press form into desired shapes. Bake at 400° about 10 minutes.

LEMON SPRITZ COOKIES

2 cups butter (1 lb)
2 cups sugar
2 egg yolks
grated rind and juice of 1 lemon
4 cups sifted flour
¼ cups chopped almonds

Cream butter and sugar until light. Add egg yolks and beat. Add rind and lemon juice and mix. Add flour and nuts and mix well. Using cookie press, bake on lightly greased cookie sheets at 400° for about 8 to 10 minutes. Also good with a thin powdered sugar frosting, colored.

STRUDEL PARTY SLICES

3 cups sifted cake flour
1 cup butter
2 Tbs sugar
2 egg yolks
½ cup milk
1 ounce yeast

Dissolve yeast in warm milk. Let stand for 25 minutes while mixing dough. Blend butter with flour. Add beaten egg yolks with sugar and beat well. Add yeast mixture and continue beating very well. Cover with waxed paper and refrigerate overnight. Roll out thin on floured board. Take small amounts of dough at a time. Spread with following filling.

FILLING

½ cup chopped pecans
2 Tbs cinnamon
1 cup sugar

Roll as for jelly roll, brush with 2 beaten egg whites. Spread on filling. Bake in 350° oven for about 15 minutes. Slice in 1 inch slices when cool. Dust with conf. sugar.

SUSAN'S COOKIES

1 cup butter
½ cup sugar
3 egg yolks
1½ tsp vanilla
1 tsp baking powder
1 cup chopped nuts
2 cups flour
¼ tsp salt

Cream butter and sugar until light and fluffy. Add egg yolks and vanilla. Mix well. Add sifted dry ingredients and mix. Mix in chopped nuts. Roll into small balls. Dip into slightly beaten egg white and top each with colored cherries or ¼ gumdrop. Bake on greased cookie sheets at 350° 25 to 30 minutes.

MOM'S OLD FASHIONED SUGAR COOKIES

1 cup soft butter
1½ cups sugar
½ tsp salt
2 eggs, beaten
1 tsp vanilla
¼ tsp almond extract
½ tsp baking soda
3 Tbs sweet cream
3 cups sifted flour

Combine first 6 ingredients and mix well. Mix until light and fluffy. Dissolve soda in cream. Add to creamed mixture and mix very well. Gradually beat in flour. Mix well. Wrap in waxed paper and chill. Roll out on lightly floured board about 1/8 inch thick. Roll small amounts at a time, keeping rest of dough in refrigerator. Cut into desired shapes. Place on ungreased cookie sheets and bake in 375° oven from 8 to 10 minutes. Sprinkle with granulated or colored sugar.

Not enough sugar gives a flat tasting product with a bread-like texture.

SWEDISH DELIGHTS

¼ tsp ammonium carbonate (crushed)
   (available in drug stores)
1½ tsp vanilla

Combine and let stand.

1 cup butter
1 cup sugar
1 cup shortening
3 cups flour
¼ tsp salt
2 cups moist coconut short thread

Cream butter, sugar and shortening. Add flour sifted with salt. Mix well. Add coconut. Mix well. Add vanilla mixture. Chill until able to handle. Roll in balls size of a walnut. Bake on ungreased cookie sheet until brown about 10 minutes. Bake at 350° to 375°. Decorate with cherry.

ORANGE TEA COOKIES

1 cup butter
1 cup sugar
1 egg
1 tsp grated orange rind
2 Tbs orange juice
2 cups sifted flour

Cream butter and sugar until light and fluffy. Add well beaten egg and mix well. Add orange rind and juice. Mix well. Add sifted flour. Chill dough for a few hours. Roll dough thin on a floured board and cut with small round cutter. Bake on greased cookie sheets in 400° oven for about 6 minutes. When cool frost ½ of the cookies with orange frosting. Cover with remaining cookies.

ORANGE FROSTING

1¾ cup plus 2 Tbs sifted conf. sugar
3 Tbs orange juice
3 Tbs melted butter
1½ tsp grated orange rind

Mix all ingredients well and put between two cookies.

FAVORITE TEA COOKIES

1 cup butter
½ cup conf. sugar
1 tsp vanilla
2¼ cups sifted flour
¼ tsp salt
¾ cup chopped nuts

Cream butter, add sugar, add vanilla. Mix well. Add flour and salt and nuts. Mix well. Form into small balls. Place on ungreased cookie sheet. Bake at 400° 10 to 15 minutes. Roll in conf. sugar while hot, again when cool.

SWISS COCONUT BALLS

4 egg whites
1 cup conf. sugar
2 cups moist coconut
½ cup flour
1 tsp vanilla

Beat egg whites until stiff. Add vanilla and sugar gradually. Add flour and coconut. Mix well. Drop an inch apart on greased and floured cookie sheet. Bake at 350° 15 minutes. Remove at once with spatula and cool on racks.

TEA DAINTIES

2½ cups sifted flour
½ tsp salt
¼ tsp cinnamon
1 cup soft butter
1 3 ounce package cream cheese
1 cup sugar
1 egg yolk
1 tsp vanilla extract
1 tsp grated orange rind

Cream butter and cream cheese well. Add sugar gradually and mix well until light and fluffy. Add egg yolk, vanilla and orange rind, mixing well. Add sifted dry ingredients and mix well. Using a cookie press form into desired shapes on greased baking sheets. Bake in 350° oven for about 12 minutes. Will make about 5 or 6 dozen cookies.

RICH TEA COOKIES

2½ cups sifted flour
½ tsp salt
1 cup butter
⅔ cup sugar
3 egg yolks
½ tsp vanilla
½ cup grated almonds

Mix and sift flour and salt. Cream butter well. Add sugar gradually. Add vanilla, egg yolks and nuts and mix well. Add flour mixture. Mix very well. Roll ¼ inch thick. Cut in desired shapes. Press a nut-meat half in center of each cookie. Bake at 375° about 9 or 10 minutes.

TINY TOFFEE SQUARES

2 cups sifted flour
½ tsp salt
1 cup butter
1 tsp vanilla
1 cup dark brown sugar sifted and packed
1 egg

Cream butter and sugar until light and fluffy. Add well beaten egg and vanilla and mix well. Add sifted ingredients gradually and mix well. Spread batter in a shallow pan about 10x15 inches. Bake at 350° for 20 minutes. Spread with following while warm:
½ pound German sweet chocolate, melted. Sprinkle with ground nuts.

TOM THUMB BARS

Mix together and bake

½ cup butter
1 cup flour
½ cup brown sugar

Pat in 13x9x2 inch greased pan in 325° oven for 15 minutes.

Mix

2 eggs
1 cup brown sugar
2 Tbs flour
¼ tsp salt
1 cup chopped nuts
1½ cup coconut
1 tsp vanilla

Spread on baked crust. Bake at 325° for 25 minutes. Cut into bars when cool.

TROBIES

1 cup butter or shortening
1 cup sugar
½ cup sour milk
1 tsp soda
1 tsp vanilla
½ tsp salt
3 cups quick oatmeal
2 cups flour

Cream butter and sugar well. Add sour milk and vanilla. Mix well. Add sifted flour and soda. Mix well. Add oats beating well. Roll out thin on floured board and cut with small round cookie cutter. Bake in 350° oven until brown, about 10 minutes. When cool fill with the following filling.

FILLING

2 cups raisins
Water to cover
1 cup sugar

Cook slowly and mash. Cool and fill cookies like sandwiches. Dust with conf. sugar if desired. Press with tines of fork. Cooked dates or apricot filling can also be used.

VIRGINIA COOKIES

¾ cup shortening
½ cup sugar
1 egg yolk
2 cups sifted cake flour
1 tsp vanilla

Cream shortening and sugar well. Add egg yolk and beat well. Add flour a little at a time. Add vanilla, beating well. Shape into small balls. May also be put through a cookie press. Bake on greased cookie sheets in 375° to 400° oven from 4 to 6 minutes.

VIENNESE TREATS

1 cup butter
1 cup sugar
2 egg yolks
1 tsp grated lemon rind
2 cups sifted flour
¾ tsp cinnamon
½ tsp cloves
1 cup grated almonds

Cream butter and sugar until light and fluffy. Add egg yolks, nuts and lemon rind and mix well. Add sifted dry ingredients and mix well. Roll ¼ inch thick on floured board and cut with cookie cutters dipped in flour. Bake on very lightly greased cookie sheets in a 350° oven, until brown. About 10 or 15 minutes.

WALNUT BUTTER COOKIES

1½ cups sifted flour
½ cup sugar
¼ tsp salt
2 tsp instant coffee
1 cup butter
¾ cup chopped walnuts

Sift into mixing bowl, flour, sugar, salt and instant coffee. With pastry blender cut in butter until mixture resembles small peas. Press dough together. Shape into small balls and roll in chopped nuts. Place on greased cookie sheets and flatten with glass dipped in sugar. Bake at 300° for about 20 minutes or until the edges are lightly browned. Cool slightly before removing from sheets.

No Sour Milk?

Add 1 Tbs. of lemon juice or vinegar to cup of sweet milk. Let stand for 15 minutes.

WALNUT BARS

½ cup butter
1 cup sifted flour

Blend butter and flour well and pat evenly in a greased pan (7½ by 13½ inches). Bake in 350° oven about 15 minutes.

Second part:

½ cup dry coconut
1½ cups brown sugar sifted and packed
1 cup chopped walnuts
2 Tbs flour
¼ tsp baking powder
½ tsp salt
2 eggs, well beaten
1½ tsp vanilla

Mix all ingredients well and spread on baked layer. Bake in 350° oven . . . about 25 minutes. Cool. Frost with conf. sugar frosting and sprinkle with ground nuts.

JUICE FROSTING

2 Tbs melted butter
1¾ tsp lemon juice
2 Tbs orange juice
1½ cups sifted conf. sugar

Add melted butter and juices to sugar and mix well.

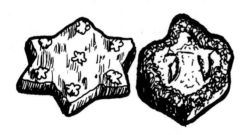

WALNUT SURPRISES

1 cup butter
¾ cup brown sugar
1 egg yolk
1 tsp vanilla
2 cups sifted flour
Walnut halves

Cream butter and sugar until light and fluffy. Add egg yolk and vanilla and mix. Add flour and mix well. Using about 1 tsp of dough, make a little pattie in the palm of your hand and put a walnut half in center of pattie. Fold over to form a cookie. Be sure all of the walnut half is covered. Place on greased cookie sheets and flatten slightly with tines of fork. Brush with slightly beaten egg white. Top with small piece of candied cherry. Bake at about 375° for 8 to 10 minutes.

HEAVENLY WALNUT COOKIES

½ cup butter
½ cup sugar
1 egg white unbeaten
¾ cup chopped walnuts
1 cup sifted flour
1 tsp baking powder
½ tsp salt
1 egg yolk
1 Tbs water (cold)

Cream butter and sugar until light and fluffy. Add egg white, nuts, and sifted dry ingredients. Mix very well. Roll on floured board 1/8 inch thick. Cut with cooky cutters. Brush tops of cookies with the egg yolk mixed with water. Bake on ungreased cookie sheets about 10 to 12 minutes until a delicate brown at 375°.

CHRISTMAS ALMOND WREATHS

1 cup butter
¾ cup conf. sugar
1 tsp vanilla
2 egg yolks
1 egg white
2 cups sifted flour
¼ tsp salt
½ cup ground almonds
2 Tbs sugar
candied cherries

Sift together flour and salt. Cream butter and sugar and vanilla until light and fluffy. Add egg yolks and beat well. Stir in dry ingredients and mix well. Put through cookie press onto ungreased cookie sheet using rosette tube to form wreaths. Brush with egg white. Sprinkle with ground almonds and sugar. Trim with ground or chopped candied cherries if desired. Bake at 350° for 8 to 10 minutes.

CHRISTMAS BUTTER BALLS

1 cup butter
2 teaspoons vanilla
⅓ cup granulated sugar
2 teaspoons water
2 cups flour
1 cup chopped pecans or walnuts
red or green sugar or colored candies

Cream butter, sugar and vanilla. Add water and mix. Add flour stirring thoroughly. Fold in nuts and mix until dough is of uniform consistency. Shape into small balls the size of a walnut. Roll in colored sugar. Place onto ungreased cookie sheet about 1 inch apart. Bake at 325° 25 minutes.

Varieties that have a large amount of fat or large amounts of nuts may become rancid. Do not use stale nuts.

CHRISTMAS LOGS

2½ cups sifted flour
½ cup conf. sugar
¼ tsp salt
¾ cup shortening
½ cup light molasses
1 tsp vanilla
1 cup chopped nuts

Blend flour, sugar and salt. Cut in shortening, stir in molasses and vanilla and mix well. Chill dough for about one hour. Shape into small logs about 2 inches long and ½ inch thick. Roll in chopped nuts and bake on an ungreased cookie sheet. Bake at 325° from 10 to 15 minutes. Makes about 5 dozen.

CHRISTMAS TREES

⅔ cup butter or shortening
¾ cup sugar
2 eggs
1 tsp lemon juice
1 tsp lemon rind, grated
2 cups sifted flour
½ tsp salt
1½ tsp baking powder

Cream butter and sugar until light and fluffy. Add eggs, lemon juice and grated lemon rind. Mix well. Add sifted dry ingredients and beat well. Chill dough. Roll out 1/8 inch thick on floured board. Cut in shapes of trees or stars. Brush with slightly beaten egg white. Sprinkle with colored sugar. Also can be frosted. Temperature 375°—8 to 10 minutes.

BOHEMIAN CHRISTMAS COOKIES

1 cup butter
1¼ cup sifted conf. sugar
1 tsp vanilla
pinch salt
1½ bars or 6 ounches grated German
   sweet choc.
2¼ cups sifted flour
1 cup chopped walnuts

Cream butter and sugar until light and fluffy. Add all remaining ingredients and mix well. Chill for several hours. Shape into small balls. Place on ungreased cookie sheet and bake at 375° for 12 to 15 minutes. Dust with powdered sugar when cool.

BERLINER KRANZER NO. 1

4 hard cooked egg yolks
2 cups conf. sugar
4 raw egg yolks
½ tsp vanilla
½ tsp almond extract
2 cups butter
5 to 6 cups sifted flour
slightly beaten egg white
granulated sugar

Put hard cooked egg yolks through a sieve. Work in sugar. Add raw egg yolks, beaten. Add the flavoring and the butter and the flour. Mix well. Chill dough. Using a cookie press, form into desired shapes. Can also be made into small wreath like cookies round as a pencil. Dip into slightly beaten egg whites and sprinkle with sugar. Bake in 375° oven for about 8 or 10 minutes.

BERLINER KRANZER NO. 2

4 hard cooked egg yolks
1 cup butter
1 cup sugar
chopped nuts
4 raw egg yolks
1 cup cream
4 cups flour

Put hard cooked egg yolks through a sieve. Set aside. Cream butter, add sugar and mix well. Beat in 4 raw egg yolks, one at a time. Mix well. Add the hard cooked yolks and sifted flour with cream. Mix well.

These cookies may be refrigerated in rolls and sliced. May also be rolled and cut into desired shapes, and sprinkled with sugar. May also be put through a cookie press. Brush the rolled cookies with egg white before the sugar is sprinkled on. Also sprinkle with nuts. Bake on slightly greased cookie sheets at 425° for 10 minutes.

BLACK WALNUT CHRISTMAS COOKIES

1¾ cup butter
½ cup sugar
2¼ cups brown sugar sifted and packed
2 eggs
1½ cups black walnuts
6 cups sifted flour
1 tsp salt
½ tsp soda
1 tsp cream of tartar
2 tsp vanilla
1½ cups shredded coconut

Cream butter and sugars until light and fluffy. Add eggs and vanilla and mix well. Grind nuts and coconut together with fine blade on food chopper. Electric blender can also be used. Add to creamed mixture and blend well. Add sifted dry ingredients and mix well. Chill dough. Shape into rolls (4) about 2 inches in diameter. Wrap in waxed paper and chill for several hours. Cut into 1/8 inch slices and baked on greased cookie sheets about 10 to 12 minutes. 350° to 375°.

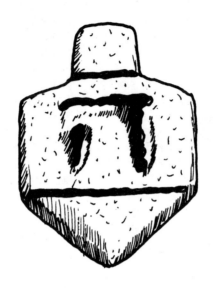

HOLIDAY KISSES

3 egg whites
1/8 tsp salt
½ tsp cream of tartar
2¼ cups sifted conf. sugar
1 tsp vanilla
2 cups chopped pecans

Beat egg whites with rotary beater until foamy. Add salt and cream of tartar slowly and continue beating until egg whites are stiff and stand in peaks. Add sugar gradually, beating well. Add vanilla and mix. Fold in chopped nuts. Drop by spoonfuls on lightly greased cookie sheets. Bake at 300° about 15 to 20 minutes. Store in air-tight container.

HOLIDAY ROUNDS

½ cup butter
¼ cup brown sugar
1 egg yolk, beaten
1 cup flour
1½ tsp vanilla
¾ cup ground nuts
1 egg white, unbeaten

Cream butter and sugar, add egg yolk beaten. Add vanilla, blend in flour. Mix well. Roll in small balls. Dip in unbeaten egg white, then in nuts . . . or roll in colored sugar. Bake on greased cookie sheet in slow oven. 300°—20 minutes.

HOLIDAY POPPY SEED COOKIES

1 cup butter
½ cup sugar
¼ tsp salt
2 egg yolks
2 cups sifted flour
3 Tbs poppy seeds
semi-sweet chocolate bits
1 tsp vanilla

Cream butter, sugar and salt until light and fluffy. Add vanilla and egg yolks one at a time and mix well. Stir in flour and mix well. Mix in poppy seeds. Shape into small balls. Place on lightly greased cookie sheets about 1 inch apart. Press in center of each cookie with thumb. Bake at 375° for 10 to 12 minutes. Remove from cookie sheets and cool. Press in center again when cool. Fill centers with melted semi-sweet chocolate bits.

HONEY BRAN CHRISTMAS COOKIES

½ cup butter
½ cup honey
½ cup All-Bran
2 cups sifted all-purpose flour
1 tsp baking soda
½ tsp cinnamon
¼ tsp cloves
½ tsp allspice
Colored sugar

Blend butter with honey and beat until creamy. Crush All-Bran slightly. Sift together flour, soda and spices. Add to honey mixture with All-Bran. Mix thoroughly. Chill. Roll dough on lightly floured board to about 1/16 inch in thickness. Cut into angels. Place on greased cookie sheets. Bake in 350° oven for about 10 minutes. Yield: about 4 dozen assorted cookies.

KRINGLER

2 cups flour
1 cup butter
3½ Tbs cream
2 egg yolks
½ cup chopped nuts

Blend flour and butter, same as you would for pastry. Add the cream and egg yolks. Handle as little as possible. Mix. Chill dough for at least 1 hour. Roll to about ¼ inch thickness. Sprinkle with chopped nuts and a little sugar. Cut into stripes about 4 or 5 inches long and shape into a pretzel-like cookie. Stripe should be about ½ inch wide. Place on greased cookie sheets and bake at 350° to 375° 15 to 20 minutes. Cookies should be light brown.

KRIS KRINGLES

1 cup butter
½ cup sugar
2 egg yolks
2 Tbs grated orange rind
2 tsp grated lemon rind
1 tsp lemon juice
2 cups cake flour
¼ tsp salt
chopped nuts
candied cherries

Cream butter and sugar, add egg yolks, orange and lemon rind and juice. Mix well. Stir in flour and salt. Beat well. Chill dough. Shape into small balls, and dip into beaten egg whites. Roll lightly in nuts, ground. Press a piece of candied cherry in center of each cookie. Bake at 350° for 20 minutes.

MANDEL KRANZE

½ cup butter
⅓ cup sugar
1 egg white
2 Tbs sugar
1 egg yolk
1¼ cup sifted flour
1 tsp cinnamon
¼ cup chopped almonds

Cream butter and sugar ⅓ cup until light and fluffy. Add beaten egg yolk and mix well. Add flour gradually and mix well. Roll thin on floured board, cut with round cutter. Brush with beaten egg white and sprinkle with mixture of the 2 Tbs sugar, cinnamon and nuts. Bake in 400° oven for about 8 or 9 minutes.

Holiday cookies and cakes in which honey is used need about two weeks to ripen. They improve with age, provided they are stored in covered jars in a cool place. Regular fruit jars with rubber rings may also be used.

MEXICAN CHRISTMAS COOKIES

3 cups sifted flour
1 tsp salt
1 tsp ginger
1 tsp cinnamon
1 tsp cloves
6 ounces pitted dates, cut fine
   (about 1 1/8 cups)
1 cup chopped pecans
1 cup butter
2 cups sugar
3 eggs
3 Tbs milk
1 tsp baking soda

Mix flour, salt and spices; add dates and nuts and mix. Cream butter, add sugar gradually and cream until fluffy. Add well-beaten eggs and mix. Add milk in which soda has been dissolved and mix well. Add flour mixture gradually and mix. Form dough into rolls, about 2 inches in diameter, wrap in waxed paper and freeze or chill thoroughly in refrigerator. Slice thin and bake on ungreased baking sheets in preheated 375° oven about 12 minutes. Store in covered container. Yield: About 6 dozen.

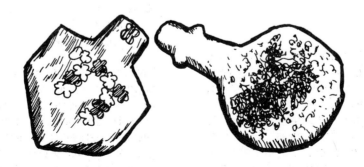

RICH FLAVOR CHRISTMAS COOKIES

1 cup butter
½ cup sugar
1 egg, unbeaten
2 tsp vanilla
3 cups sifted flour
½ tsp baking powder
1/8 tsp salt

Cream butter and sugar thoroughly. Add egg and vanilla. Mix well. Gradually stir in sifted dry ingredients until well blended. Chill if needed to make easier to handle. Roll small amounts of dough 1/8 inch thick on a floured board. Shape with cookie cutters as desired. Bake on ungreased cookie sheet at 350° about 10 or 12 minutes or until delicately browned.

SPRINGERLE

2 cups sifted flour
1 tsp baking powder
¼ tsp salt
About 4 or 5 drops anise ext.
2 eggs
1 cup sugar

Beat eggs until light, add sugar and beat until light and fluffy. Add sifted dry ingredients with anise flavoring and mix well. Roll out with Springerle rolling pin on floured board. Sprinkle rolling pin with flour if necessary. Cut into squares and allow to dry on board overnight. Bake on well greased cookie sheet at 325° for about 15 minutes. Store in covered container.

SANTA CLAUS COOKIES

3¾ cups sifted flour
1¼ tsp baking powder
2½ tsp cinnamon
1¼ tsp cloves
1½ cups butter
2 cups brown sugar, sifted and packed
1 egg

Mix and sift flour, baking powder and spices. Cream butter, add sugar gradually and cream until fluffy; add egg and mix. Add sifted dry ingredients gradually and mix. Chill in refrigerator. Roll about 1/8 inch thick and cut out with assorted floured cutters. Bake on ungreased baking sheets in preheated 350° oven about 12 minutes. Store in covered container. Yield: 6 dozen.

SOUR CREAM HOLIDAY COOKIES

1 cup shortening
2 cups brown sugar
1 egg well beaten
1 cup sour cream
½ tsp soda
¼ tsp salt
4½ cups flour
1 tsp baking powder

Cream shortening and sugar. Add well beaten eggs and mix well. Add sifted dry ingredients alternately with cream, to which has been added 1½ tsp vanilla. Roll on floured board. Cut with cookie cutter in desired shapes. Bake at 400° 8 to 10 minutes.

SUSAN'S FAVORITE CHRISTMAS COOKIES

2 cups butter
2 cups powdered sugar
Juice of one lemon
4 tsp vanilla
3 cups sifted flour
½ pound almonds
blanched and put through the
finest chopper.

Cream butter, sugar, vanilla and lemon juice until light and fluffy. Add flour and almonds and mix well. Refrigerate overnight for easier handling. Shape into small balls the size of a walnut. Flatten to ½ inch thickness. Bake on very lightly greased cookie sheet 350° about 10 or 15 minutes or until lightly brown around the edges. Dust with powdered sugar when cool.

SWEDISH CHRISTMAS COOKIES

6 egg yolks (hard boiled)
2 cups sifted flour
½ tsp salt
¾ cup butter
¾ cup sugar
½ tsp lemon extract
1 Tbs light cream

Cream butter and sugar until light and fluffy. Add lemon flavoring and hard cooked egg yolks which have been put through a sieve. Mix well. Blend in cream and sifted dry ingredients and mix well. Chill dough for a few hours. Roll out to 1/8 inch thickness and cut into desired shapes. Place on greased cookie sheets and bake at 375° for 5 to 8 minutes. These can be decorated with colored sugar before baking or frosted if desired.

ALASKAN CHOCOLATE FROSTING

1 cup powdered sugar
¼ cup milk (scant)
1 egg
2 sqs. chocolate melted with 3 Tbs butter
¾ tsp salt

Use electric mixer if possible. Put small bowl into large size bowl surrounded by ice cubes. Add ingredients in order given above, making sure chocolate mixture is cooled. Beat, using high speed. The longer you beat, the lighter the frosting becomes, five minutes should be sufficient. Cake should be cool when frosted. May also be used for filling.

BROWNED BUTTER FROSTING

Brown ½ cup butter over low heat. Remove from heat and blend in 2 cups conf. sugar, 1 tsp. vanilla and 2 Tbs milk. Beat well and use. Will cover bars made in jelly roll pan.

CHOCOLATE CREAM FROSTING

16 oz. package chocolate bits (1 cup), melted
2 Tbs butter
1 egg yolk
1½ cups conf. sugar (sifted)
¼ cup milk

Combine and mix until smooth and of spreading consistency.

CHOCOLATE FROSTING

½ cup sugar
2 Tbs cornstarch
1 oz. chocolate, cut up
½ tsp salt
½ cup boiling water
1½ Tbs butter
½ tsp vanilla extract

Mix sugar, cornstarch, chocolate, and salt in a saucepan; add boiling water. Stir and cook over low heat until glossy and smooth. About 5 minutes. Add butter and extract and mix well.

COCOA FROSTING

3 Tbs soft butter
1 cup conf. sugar
2 Tbs cocoa
1½ Tbs cold coffee
½ to 1 tsp vanilla

Cream butter and sugar. Blend in remaining ingredients. Beat well.

CONFECTIONERS SUGAR FROSTING

1 Tbs & 1 tsp butter
¼ cup hot milk
about 3 to 3¼ cups sifted conf. sugar
1 tsp vanilla extract
food coloring

Add butter to the milk. Add sugar gradually to make frosting right for spreading. Add extract and mix well. Add food coloring as desired.

COCONUT MARSHMALLOW FROSTING

¼ cup boiling water
1 cup miniature marshmallows
2 Tbs butter
1 cup grated coconut

Combine boiling water, marshmallows, and butter. Cook over low heat until marshmallows are melted. Stir in coconut and spread on cooled baked cookies. Good on any cookies.

DECORATING ICING

1 lb. sifted conf. sugar
3 medium egg whites

Use electric mixer. Mix thoroughly, and add ½ tsp vanilla. Add more powdered sugar if needed.

COFFEE FROSTING

¼ cup butter
1 egg yolk
¼ tsp vanilla
1½ tsp instant coffee
1 Tbs cream
2 to 2½ cups confectioners sugar

Cream butter until soft. Add ½ cup sugar and beat. Add egg yolk, vanilla, coffee and cream. A little at a time until thick enough for spreading.

DECORATORS ICING

2 egg whites
1/8 tsp cream of tartar
2 tsp water
2½ to 3 cups conf. sugar

Blend egg whites, cream of tartar, and water. Beat until frothy. Gradually add sugar. Beat until mixture holds soft peaks. Tint as desired with food coloring. May also be put through decorators tube or spread with spatula.

FABULOUS FROSTING

5 Tbs flour
1 cup milk

Cook together over slow flame. Stir constantly. Cool.

Cream together well:

1 cup sugar
1 cup butter
1 tsp vanilla

Add to flour and milk mixture. Cream until light and fluffy. If a colored icing is wanted, add a few drops of food coloring. Beat before adding too much coloring in order to obtain the right color.

FLUFFY COCOA FROSTING

¼ cup butter
1½ cups conf. sugar
⅓ cup sifted cocoa
½ tsp vanilla
1 tsp cream
1 egg white

Cream butter. Add 1 cup of conf. sugar and mix well. Add cocoa and vanilla. Mix until light and fluffy. Beat egg white until stiff and add rest of sugar. Add to butter mixture and mix well.

Excess flour makes a dry crumbly cookie and in some degree conceals the flavoring qualities of the other ingredients.

HOT MILK FROSTING

1 Tbs butter
¼ cup hot milk
1 tsp vanilla
Food coloring desired
About 3 cups conf. sugar

Add butter to milk, add sugar gradually; mix well. Add vanilla and food coloring. Mix until smooth.

MAPLE CREAM FILLING

4 egg yolks
¾ cup conf. sugar
¾ cup milk
½ cup butter
2 tsp maple flavoring

Beat egg yolks until thick and lemon colored; add sugar and milk. Cook in double boiler stirring constantly until thick, about 10 minutes. Cool. Cream butter until fluffy. Add Cold custard and flavoring; beat with rotary beater until smooth. Frost and fill, 3-8 inch layer.

ORANGE FROSTING

1¾ cup plus 2 Tbs sifted conf. sugar
3 Tbs orange juice
3 Tbs melted butter
1½ tsp grated orange rind

Mix all ingredients well and put between two cookies.

QUICK BUTTER ICING FOR SPREADING

Cream ¼ cup butter; add 1 Tbs cream, ½ tsp vanilla, and about 1¼ cups confectioners' sugar or enough to form consistency for spreading. Beat well about 5 minutes.

QUICK CHOCOLATE ICING, GLOSSY

1½ Tbs hot milk
1 Tbs soft butter
1 tsp vanilla
About 1 cup conf. sugar
1 oz. melted unsweetened chocolate

Combine milk with butter and vanilla. Add sugar and vanilla to milk and butter mixture. Beat until smooth, then add melted chocolate. Mix thoroughly. Let stand about 10 or 15 minutes. If icing appears thick and dull before spreading on cake, add a few drops of milk. If too thin, add more sifted confectioners' sugar.

QUICK CHOCOLATE FROSTING

Combine:

½ cup evaporated milk
1/8 tsp salt

Bring to a boil.

Stir in:

1 cup chocolate bits
1 tsp vanilla

Mix well. Cool. Ready to use.

RUM FROSTING

3 Tbs melted butter
3 cups conf. sugar
2 Tbs cream
3 Tbs plus 1 tsp rum

Mix all ingredients well.

SOUR CREAM FROSTING

1 cup commercial sour cream
2 cups sifted powdered sugar
1 tsp grated orange or lemon rind

Combine ingredients and beat until fluffy. Spread on cooled baked cookies.

Liquids may be varied in amounts with less change in the finished product than any of the other basic ingredients. More liquid may be added to the rolled cookie dough and a drop made from the same recipe. Or less liquid may be used in a spread wafer and a rolled wafer made instead.

Variations in basic proportions will produce as many different effects as there are variations. Many are not displeasing, but all too frequently the result is a poor cookie. The right proportions depend on a good recipe to start with and upon accurate measurements.

Sugar sprinkled over the cookie before putting them in the oven forms a sweet crust and makes a richer cookie.

CHOCOLATE FILLING FOR TARTS, SMALL CAKES, BAR COOKIES, AND SANDWICH COOKIES

16 oz. package semi-sweet chocolate
  bits
½ cup sweetened condensed milk
1 Tbs butter
¼ tsp salt

Melt over hot water in a double boiler, making sure the water does not boil over into the pan holding ingredients. Remove from heat and add ½ cup chopped pecans or walnuts and 1 tsp vanilla. Mix well. Cool and use.

DATE FILLING

½ lb. dates, pitted and cut up small
½ cup sugar
½ cup water
⅓ cup nuts chopped (optional)

Cook dates, sugar and water until thickened, stirring constantly. Add nuts and mix. May also add 1 tsp lemon juice.

LEMON CREAM FILLING

1 egg, slightly beaten
Grated rind of 1 lemon
⅔ cup sugar
3 Tbs lemon juice
1½ Tbs soft butter

Cook ingredients in top of double boiler or heavy pan. Cook until thick, stirring constantly. Set aside to cool. Very tart and delicious.

WHIPPED CREAM FILLING—BASIC

½ tsp plain gelatin
1 Tbs cold water
¼ tsp vanilla
½ cup heavy cream
3 Tbs conf. sugar

Soften gelatin in cold water. Stir until dissolved over boiling water. Mix with sugar and vanilla, and cream. Whip until stiff. Chill thoroughly before spreading, two 9" layers. **Chocolate Filling** — increase sugar to 4 Tbs; mix with 2 Tbs cocoa before adding cream. **Coffee Filling** — Substitute coffee for water. **Pineapple Filling** — omit vanilla, decrease cream to ⅓ cup. Before chilling fold in ½ cup **drained** crushed pineapple. **Applesauce Filling** — Omit vanilla; decrease cream to ⅓ cup before chilling fold in ½ cup chilled thick applesauce and ½ tsp cinnamon.

SUBSTITUTIONS
READ CAREFULLY—

1. If a recipe calls for butter specifically that cookie is best made with butter and not a substitute — either flavor or texture may be impaired. If for any reason you cannot use butter, choose a recipe calling for either shortening, margarine, or oil. NEVER substitute **oil** for shortening of any kind or vice versa.

2. **EGGS** — Never substitute for eggs. Use a recipe that is eggless. There are many.

3. **SUGARS** — Brown sugar **firmly** packed may be substituted for granulated or vice versa. **Do not** substitute in recipes calling for **powdered sugar. Never** substitute synthetic sweeteners for sugar in cookies or frostings.

4. **FLOUR** — In recipes calling for **cake flour,** you may substitute all purpose flour, using **2 Tablespoons** less per cup of the amount specified in the recipe.

5. **LIQUIDS** — Coffee, fruit, juices or other liquids may generally be used with success for all or part of the liquid called for in a recipe. Evaporated milk, diluted with an equal part of water, may be used instead of fresh milk. **Liquified** powdered milk may also be used. **Never** substitute in recipes calling for sweetened condensed milk.

6. **CHOCOLATE** — In recipes calling for unsweetened bar chocolate, you may substitute cocoa using **2 and ½ Tbs.** for **1 and ½ tsps.** additional fat, for each ounce or square of chocolate.

7. **SPICES** — Salt or flavorings may be omitted from any recipe for reasons of your own. Any spice or flavoring may be added to any recipe according to your taste.

8. **NUTS, ETC.** — In any recipe, nuts may be added or omitted at your will, except when they are a major ingredient — for instance — in a nut cookie — which may leave a very bland texturless cookie. This is also true of dried fruits such as raisins, dates or figs, grated coconut, grated orange or lemon rind, ready to eat cereals and chocolate bits. If the amount called for is more than ½ cup, then do not omit the ingredients. In a recipe with 2 to 3 cups of flour about ½ cup dried fruits or nuts may safely be added. A teaspoon and a half of orange or lemon rind gives sufficient flavor to a standard size batch of cookies.

IF IN DOUBT, DO NOT SUBSTITUTE.

HINTS AND SHORT-CUTS FOR
BAKING COOKIES

1. Have all utensils ready — in one large pan.

2. Butter should be soft and eggs should be at room temperature.

3. Have all decorating materials ready — nuts ground, cherries or fruit cut into desired pieces.

4. Put ground nuts into strainer — the dust is to be used for decorating.

5. Put nuts, chopped or ground, into jars and label them. Saves time.

6. Be sure to use pan specified in recipe.

7. Medium sized eggs are best.

8. When substituting cake flour for regular flour, add 2 more tbsps. of cake flour for each cup of flour in recipe.

9. If Spritz dough is not soft enough, add one unbeaten egg white or a little cream.

10. Place butter cookie dough in refrigerator for a short time for easier handling, if necessary.

11. For Ice-box cookies, do not let dough get too cold — cookies will crack when ready to cut. Remove from refrigerator a short time before baking, ½ hour to 45 minutes.

12. Be sure and use sharp knife for cutting ice-box cookies.

13. Remove cookies with a spatula to prevent them from breaking.

14. When using maraschino cherries for decorating, be sure all the juice is drained.

15. Mark off bar cookies to size wanted while they are still hot.

16. Cut down when cool — not cold.

17. Be sure to have a moist sponge handy — also hand towel.

18. Place cookies to cool on wire cake rack. That will prevent moisture to accumulate.

19. Do not overbake cookies, they get too dry and crisp.

20. Use floured hands for patting dough in bar pans. Go over dough with rolling pin.

21. Cookie dough is much softer when using an electric mixer. Sometimes a little extra flour may have to be added.

22. When pastry flour is called for, use ½ recipe regular and ½ recipe cake flour.

23. Be sure to add eggs one at a time, beating them well after each addition, to avoid curdling.

24. When using a rolling pin, be sure it is cleaned of excess dough at all times.

25. Flour may or may not be sifted. It is best to spoon flour into measuring cup.

HINTS ON PACKING, FREEZING AND
STORING COOKIES

1. All cookies should be thoroughly cooled before storing.

2. Store soft or chewy cookies, in an air tight container to keep them from becoming hard.

3. To keep crisp cookies from becoming soft and limp, store in loosely covered container in a cool dry place.

4. Always use waxed paper between layers when storing or freezing cookies.

5. Cookies can be frozen before or after baking. Either method will give excellent results.

6. Coffee cans, shortening tins, gift tin containers — or moisture-vapor proof containers are excellent for freezing cookies.

7. Bar and crisp cookies are best if defrosted in their own wrappings. Other types may be thawed unwrapped. Baked cookies thaw at room temperature in about 15 minutes.

8. Unbaked dough should be molded into shapes you desire. Rolls or in baking pans of different shapes and sizes.

9. Allow from 3 to 6 hours after removing dough from freezer before slicing to bake. Let thaw in refrigerator.

10. Cookie dough that is stored should be used in from 4 to 6 months.

11. Baked cookies can be frozen from 9 to 12 months.

12. Do not freeze doughs that contain large amounts of egg whites, or that are highly spiced. Spiced cookies, also doughs, undergo a flavor change during freezing.

13. Take time in handling your cookies—haste makes waste.

14. Always have cookies on hand for gifts, for a hospital call, or just a treat for the family or friends. Make them by the hundreds — They go fast!

STANDARD MEASURES

3 tsp.	1 tbs.
4 Tbs.	¼ cup
16 Tbs.	1 cup
2 cups	1 pint
½ pint	1 cup
1 pint	2 cups
1 quart	4 cups (2 pints)
1 gallon	4 quarts (liquid)
1 peck	4 quarts (solid)
1 bushel	4 pecks
1 pound	16 ounces

ABBREVIATIONS

tsp.	teaspoon
Tbs.	tablespoon
pt.	pint
qt.	quart
min.	minute
hr.	hour
sq.	square
med.	medium
mod.	moderate
pkg.	package
doz.	dozen
lb.	pound
c.	cup
oz.	ounce
dash	less than 1/8 teaspoon

STANDARD OVEN TEMPERATURES

Slow	250-350 degrees
Moderate	350-400 degrees
Hot	400-450 degrees
Very Hot	450-500 degrees

FOOD EQUIVALENTS

1 Lb. granulated sugar—2 cups
1 Lb. confectioners' sugar—4½ cups sifted
1 Lb. brown sugar—2 cups packed
1 Cup egg whites—8 to 11 whites
1 Cup egg yolks—about 12 yolks
1 Lb. shelled almonds—3 cups
1 Lb. shelled walnuts—4 cups
1 Lb. shelled pecans—4 cups
1 Lb. shelled peanuts—2¾ cups
1 Lb. dried apricots—3⅔ cups
1 Lb. bread flour—4 cups unsifted
1 Lb. cake flour—4½ cups unsifted
1 Lbs. lard—2 cups
1 Lb. currants—2 3/8 cups
1 Lb. butter—2 cups solidly packed
1 Lb. vegetable shortening or bland lard—
    2⅓ cups solidly packed
1 Lb. Maple sugar—1¼ cups
1 Lb. bitter chocolate—16 squares
1 Lb. dates—2 cups
1 Lb. raisins—2 cups packed
1 Lb. shredded coconut—6 cups
1 Lb. marshmallow—4 cups
1 Lb. almond paste—2 cups packed
1 Lb. cranberries—4 cups

CAPACITY OF CANNED FOOD CONTAINERS

No. 1 can	1⅓ cups
No. 1 tall	2 cups
No. 2 can	2½ cups
No. 2½ can	3½ cups
No. 3 can	4 cups
No. 5 can	7 cups
No. 10 can	12 to 12 cups
No. 300 can	1¾ cups
No. 303 can	2 cups
8 ounces	1 cup

INDEX

NOTES ON COOKIES

NOTES ON COOKIES

NOTES ON COOKIES